The Little Library of Liberal Arts

Oskar Piest, *General Editor*

[NUMBER TWENTY-EIGHT]

F. H. BRADLEY

Ethical Studies

(Selected Essays)

Ethical Studies

(*Selected Essays*)

By

F. H. BRADLEY

With an Introduction by

RALPH G. ROSS

Professor of Philosophy, New York University

1951

THE LIBERAL ARTS PRESS

NEW YORK

CONTENTS

ETHICAL STUDIES

SELECTED BIBLIOGRAPHY

Works by Bradley

Ethical Studies (1876); second edition, revised, with additional notes. Oxford, 1927.

Principles of Logic (1883); second edition, revised, with Terminal Essays. Oxford, 1922.

Appearance and Reality (1893); second edition, with appendix (1897), new edition. Oxford, 1930.

Essays on Truth and Reality. Oxford, 1914.

Collected Essays. Oxford, 1935.

Works about Bradley

Campbell, Charles Arthur. *Scepticism and Construction*. London, 1931.

Church, Ralph W. *Bradley's Dialectic*. Ithaca, New York, 1942.

Eliot, Thomas Stearns. *Francis Herbert Bradley* (1926), reprinted in T. S. Eliot, *Selected Essays*. New York, 1932.

Kagey, Rudolf, *F. H. Bradley's Logic*. New York, 1931.

Metz, Rudolf. *A Hundred Years of British Philosophy*. London, 1938.

Muirhead, John H. *The Platonic Tradition in Anglo-Saxon Philosophy*. London, 1931, chapters V-IX.

Ross, Ralph Gilbert. *Scepticism and Dogma: A Study in the Philosophy of F. H. Bradley*. New York, 1940.

Taylor, Alfred Edward. *Francis Herbert Bradley, 1846-1924*. Proceedings of the British Academy, Vol. XI, 1924-5, pp. 458-468.

INTRODUCTION

I

"It is unusual," wrote T. S. Eliot in 1926, "that a book so famous and influential should remain out of print so long as Bradley's *Ethical Studies*." Bradley apparently planned a total revision of the book before he would allow republication, but when he died he left only some notes for his revision, making no change in the essentials of his belief. A second edition, with the notes, was published in 1927, fifty-one years after the book's appearance.

Reading Bradley is always a pleasant experience, although it is sometimes mixed with exasperation. Indubitably, Bradley deserves his place in that long line of British philosophers who are masters of English prose—a line that includes Bacon, Hobbes, Berkeley, and Hume. Although he often lacks the clarity of his predecessors, Bradley has his own qualities: precision and intensity, wit that is sometimes caustic, an alteration of assurance and diffidence, and above all, a singular honesty that often startles the reader by admission of error. As with all good writers, Bradley's style brings one into the presence of the man, in his case a man always exciting, sometimes paradoxical, with a deep sense of his mission as a philosopher. Yet this man, who does not hide himself behind an impersonal mask of prose, whose style is that extension of personality that all work should be, was a recluse for most of his life, seldom seen by his colleagues, with no students, and perhaps no intimates.

It was natural enough that Bradley should seek an academic career. An older half-brother, G. G. Bradley, was Master of University College, Oxford, and later Dean of Westminster. A younger brother, A. C. Bradley, became a distinguished literary critic and foremost Shakespearian scholar. F. H. Bradley (born January 30, 1846) early showed promise of scholarship and philosophic ability but failure to take a First Class in "Greats" at Oxford, and a subsequent failure to obtain a Fellowship upset him deeply and gave him much concern for his future. In 1870, however, Merton College, Oxford, elected him to a Fellowship with life tenure, but with the traditional stipulation that it was terminable by marriage.

A description of Bradley at about this time by his sister carries conviction, even allowing for her strong prejudice in his favor.

His outward appearance was striking; he was tall and upright in carriage; well and muscularly made, singularly handsome, with large gray-blue eyes under dark eyebrows and lashes, a well-modelled forehead, mouth, and chin; his head set well on his shoulders. It certainly was an arresting face . . .

Athletic as a youth, Bradley's physical activities had been somewhat curtailed, shortly before he came to study at Oxford, by a severe attack of typhoid fever which was followed by pneumonia. But it was not until about a year after he became a Fellow of Merton that his whole mode of life was changed by a "violent inflammation of the kidneys" (never precisely diagnosed) which turned him into a lifelong invalid. We can only speculate on the changes in Bradley made by ill-health: in later years, some regarded him as sensitive and kindly; others as splenetic.

From 1871 on, although he attended college functions and concerned himself with the business and administrative affairs of Merton—junior colleagues sometimes being terrified by the mordant wit of the man rumored to be "the best mind in England" —he remained for the most part in his rooms, never teaching, seldom having guests, often leaving Oxford to avoid the cold. Indeed, his constant fear of cold and draughts raises psychological questions about Bradley which could only be answered if we had considerably more information. In any event, he was the type of invalid whose constant self-care helped him outlive his contemporaries. He died of blood-poisoning on September 18, 1924, in his 79th year, after a short illness.

As a Fellow of Merton for fifty-four years, Bradley's life story is chiefly the intellectual life recorded in his writing. Each of his books made a great stir. Bosanquet called the publication of *Ethical Studies* "an epoch-making event." When William James read *The Principles of Logic* he used the same phrase, writing: "It is surely 'epoch-making' in English philosophy." *Appearance and Reality* called forth the comment from Edward Caird that it was the greatest event since Kant, and Muirhead went even farther back in intellectual history: "... nothing like it," he wrote, in reviewing the effect of the book, "had appeared since Hume's *Treatise*." In June, 1924, Bradley's accomplishments were officially recognized by the King, who awarded him the Order of Merit, a remarkable, almost unique, tribute to an English philosopher.[1]

II

Bradley is ordinarily regarded as the most original and systematic of those British thinkers who brought German philosophy to England and opposed the dominant native tradition of empiricism. Although writers like Coleridge and Carlyle were very much influenced by German thought, it still remained for a later group to master the technical equipment of the Germans and to apply it systematically. The most important members of this group were perhaps Green (predominantly a Kantian); Bradley, Bosanquet (usually treated as Hegelians); and McTaggart (an original thinker, with some resemblance to the Left Hegelians); but there were a host of others, who held academic—and sometimes political—posts of prime importance: Stirling, Caird, Nettleship, Haldane, Muirhead, Ward, Joachim, Pringle-Pattison, Seth, Rashdall, Taylor, Hoernlé—to name only some of them. The attack that these men mounted against English empiricism and Scottish intuitionism was successful in that the rebels created a new orthodoxy and then had to fight a rear-guard action against the realists and pragmatists of another generation. What Eliot said of Bradley might be repeated by their admirers about the whole group: "He replaced a philosophy which was crude and raw and provincial by one which was, in comparison, catholic, civilized, and universal."

[1] In 1949 the Order of Merit was awarded to Bertrand Russell. The political implication is clear, since a labor government was in power.

In theory of knowledge and metaphysics, Bradley and most of the British Idealists emphasized both the creative powers of mind and the organic character of the universe, and they returned religion to eminence among "advanced" thinkers (McTaggart is a notable exception). By insisting that error and evil are results of viewing the world in its parts, but that the Whole is true and good, they became apologists for a kind of Christian theology, stated in new terms and demanding reason, not faith, for proof.

In ethics and politics they were by and large supporters of conservatism (with some exceptions, like T. H. Green). To understand this, it is important to distinguish two historical traditions: that of nature, for the most part liberal; and that of society, chiefly conservative. Although these traditions can be found in ancient thought, it is the modern world, in which the lines have been drawn somewhat differently, with which we will concern ourselves. One can pose Locke and Hegel as representatives of almost antithetical positions—traditional empiricism and idealism respectively. To regard man as a creature of nature, or of God, capable of probable knowledge of the world, assured of natural law and natural right, is basic to English empiricism. It leaves its mark on documents like the Declaration of Independence and the Rights of Man. Society, it follows, should not violate natural rights, which are universal; institutions like the state are means for living well, and if they do not serve their purposes they should be altered or abolished. The individual act of thought attains tremendous importance. By thinking, men can discover whether or not their institutions are worthy, and how, if necessary, to change them.

The general temper of this Lockean attitude is not changed by the utilitarian attack on natural law. Instead of a state of nature and natural rights, the utilitarians depend on other "universal truths" about human psychology and the rational calculation of advantage. For earlier empiricists, individual liberty is a natural, or God-given, right; for John Stuart Mill it is a supremely useful social device, necessary for good government. We cannot, according to Mill, govern well without truth, and truth is a product of that human inquiry from which no one should be barred, for he may be right. Truth is not certain, and the great advantage of scientific procedures is that they can correct error; so no matter what our social decisions, people must be free to criticize, for we may be wrong.

There is, of course, a variation on this school of nature which has a very different sound. If metaphysics, or the authority of a church, can yield absolute knowledge, then society should be reshaped in accordance with the truth, and no one should be allowed to question it. Why should error be allowed when truth is known?

The reaction against the belief in natural man gave us a belief in social man and historical man. If man as we know him is essentially natural, not social, he has not changed through history; only the institutional forms of his society have changed. But if man is essentially social, he has changed along with changes in institutions. For the school of society, man is to be understood in terms of his history, his traditions, his institutions. These contain a kind of collective wisdom, for they embody the ways in which the race has solved its problems. The individual act of thought, and to some extent the individual himself, loses importance; for the act of thought is conditioned by society and, insofar as its conclusion differs from the conventional, the accepted, it is opposing the history and the wisdom of the race.

Hume, as a Tory in politics, had intimated portions of this argument, and had paved the way for Burke. But as an empiricist, Hume had developed other theories which were used by the philosophical radicals. It was Burke, and to some extent Carlyle, who developed the conservative implications of social man in England. The Germans, especially Hegel (and in his own way, Marx) developed the full doctrine of "historicism."

Social institutions in any specified locality and time, it was maintained, are pretty much of a piece. They exhibit an underlying idea which can be discovered by examining them in their interrelations; and they are the necessary product of what preceded them. Equally, man's philosophies, his moral obligations, his artistic creations, are relative to, and integrated with, a given society and a given time.

This philosophy of society and history creates a paradox by its very statement. Is it not itself a product of a culture and an age, to be succeeded by another philosophy, equally true for its time? No, it can be answered, for it is a philosophy which explains philosophies, a sort of meta-philosophy. Its truth, then, is not relative, like the truth of other philosophies; it is absolute, and must not be superseded.

This paradox and its resolution create further doctrine. Throughout history, there is a progression toward greater and still greater self-consciousness, an accretion of wisdom, until the process itself is finally understood. In the course of this process, society moves toward absolute truth, in its outlines at least, about the universe, society, and man.

This assurance of truth in general, which does not always extend to truth in detail, is far from uncommon. People who are unsure of the laws of physics, the name of England's ruling house, and the size of the population of New York, are often sure of the nature and destiny of man, his purposes on earth, and the nature of his moral obligations. Bradley, who was honestly doubtful of many of his own conclusions, and who rejected much of the Hegelian pattern, could yet write about his doctrine of the Absolute:

Outside our main result there is nothing except the wholly unmeaning, or else something which on scrutiny is seen really not to fall outside. Thus the supposed Other will, in short, turn out to be actually the same; or it will contain elements included within our view of the Absolute, but elements dislocated and so distorted into erroneous appearance. And the dislocation itself will find a place within the limits of our system.

The approval which won Bradley the Order of Merit can perhaps be better understood in terms of this background: The British Idealists were justifying the established social order; they were sanctifying tradition by making it reasonable; in a way they were justifying all traditions by making them right for their time and place, and then adding a fillip to their self-righteousness by making theirs the best, because it was the latest.

Hegel had done the same thing for Prussia; Marx did it for those rebels who allied themselves with the society to come; Bradley did it, less explicitly, for England.

The absolute idealists, believing in the organic nature of the universe and in man as a part of the total organism, could not, however, rest entirely on society as a criterion of morals. They developed a twofold criterion based on the dual nature of man: as social and as ideal. This was an attempt to deal with man as a natural being by redefining nature so as to make it ideal, or spiritual, or experiential, and in consequence to redefine man. But the opposition between man as social and man as ideal created a new problem to be resolved dialectically on a higher level. In ethics, the problem was posed thus: man should fulfill his obligations as a member of society; he should also live up to his ideal nature; how, then, should he behave so as to reconcile the two?

Naturalism has made us familiar with the belief that man is continuous with nature, not a perceptive and purposive creature set off from a blind and mechanical matter. Bradley's attitude toward man and his relations to the world is more romantic than naturalistic. "Man," says the romantic poet John Davidson, "is the Universe become conscious." Bradley writes: "What I mean by truth and reality is that world which satisfies the claim of the Universe present in and to what I call self." And then he puts it perhaps even more strongly: "... my desire and my will to have truth is the will and the desire of the world to become truth in me. Truth is a mode of the self-realization of myself and of the Universe in one."

Bradley's belief in the continuity of the individual with the universe implies not only a special conception of the individual but also a special conception of the universe. It is as if the universe as a total structure actually strove to realize itself in the consciousness of man. That consciousness is a perspective on a common world, but it is not a perspective that can be shared directly with others; what sharing there is results from communication. The self is not to be identified with a perspective, or an individual consciousness. The self may not be distinguished, in any particular experience, from the object of that experience (as in the instance of listening to music); on the other hand the self may become its own object of thought.

We can now understand more clearly the problem of the dual nature of man. Society is not the sole criterion of morality, because man is not only a social being; he is a part of the universe as well. His obligations would be inadequately met by the performance of social duty; he has also to live up to the conditions imposed on him as a being through whom universal truth and reality strive to be realized.

III

The publication of *Ethical Studies* was a setback to the influence of the Utilitarians. It was the first full-scale work in ethics of the British Idealists and it pointed a direction which, for the most part, they took. The book contains a vigorous polemic, with all of Bradley's dialectical virtuosity in play, against both the Utilitarians and the Kantians. The Utilitarians, Bradley argued, did not understand the necessarily universal character of morals; and the Kantians understood the universal but provided it with no content. The categorical imperative urged a duty which it never defined, but it was a universal duty and Bradley tried to make it concrete.

The general principle that Bradley urged as a moral guide was self-realization. This involves the problem of the nature of the self and, as we have seen, that is twofold. One of its aspects, the nature of man as social, is the basis for criticism of the school of nature in philosophy. In the chapter, "My Station and its Duties," Bradley presents the heart of his arguments. His position is more extreme than Rousseau's. Rousseau had regarded man's humanness as being a result of society; Bradley made society necessary for man's *reality*.

. . . man is a social being; he is real only because he is social, and can realize himself only because it is as social that he realizes himself. The mere individual is a delusion of theory; and the attempt to realize it in practice is the starvation and mutilation of human nature, with total sterility or the production of monstrosities.

Each individual man has a station in society; he is not merely an anonymous member of it. Every station is individual. It is not merely that a man is a lawyer; he is this lawyer, with these clients, and a particular set of cases that he has tried. Every citizen, or subject, will have certain moral obligations just insofar as he is a citizen or subject; he will have other obligations insofar as he is a farmer, husband, father, and so on; he will have still other obligations insofar as he is himself, a specific and identifiable part of the larger network of social relations, uniquely determined by the totality of his own relations.

This leads to a position at once stoical and conservative. Every station in life has obligations which should be fulfilled. In general, fulfilling them, doing one's work in the world is good. It is shallow to raise questions about whether there should be such a station as some man occupies or whether its obligations are worthy of being fulfilled. The existence of the station is the product of a social history that embodies human wisdom. It is arrogant and pretentious to think that I, who result from that history and am formed by the institutions in which I was educated, can question their essential soundness. Bradley says: ". . . 'my station and its duties' teaches us to identify others and ourselves with the station we fill; to consider that as good, and by virtue of that to consider others and ourselves good too. It teaches us that a man who does his work in the world is good, not withstanding his faults, if his faults do not prevent him from fulfilling his station. It tells us that the heart is an idle abstraction; we are not to think of it, nor must we look at our insides, but at our work and our life, and say to ourselves, Am I fulfilling my appointed function or not? Fulfill it we can, if we will: what we have to do is not so much better than the world that we cannot do it; the world is there waiting for it; my duties are my rights."

Not only does this position dispose of the empiricists, but it also corrects the Kantians by showing how a man's specific duties can be discovered. To state the categorical imperative without qualification is for Bradley only to insist that we should fulfill undefined duties. What is to happen when a man has several duties and these conflict? Even in a particular case, what is the precise extent of our behavior in following our duty? Bradley conceives an "ordinary man" as thinking:

One should give to the poor—in what cases and how much? Should sacrifice oneself—in what way and within what limits? Should not indulge one's appetite—except when it is right. Should not idle away one's time—except when one takes one's pleasure. Nor neglect one's work—but for some good reason. All these points we admit are in one way matter of law; but if you think to decide in particular cases by applying some "categorical imperative" you must be a pedant, if not a fool.

In giving Kant's universal a particular content, Bradley has come perilously near to an identification of what *is* with what *ought to be*, so that, as with Hegel or Marx, it is almost impossible to avoid the conclusion that what is, is right. Bradley did not even have the philosophical justification of an elaborate philosophy of history which, like Hegel's or Marx's (or for that matter St. Augustine's), makes the good an inevitable outcome of historical development. He was not committed to the doctrine that what exists is necessary and what is necessary is right. His conservatism is more like Burke's: a belief in the wisdom of existing institutions and social relationships. But, with Hegel, Bradley believed in the organic character of society as well as the organic character of the world.

The second aspect of man's nature is what saves him from a necessary acceptance of all that is conventional. As a part of the organic universe, man has other duties than those to society. Not only does the universe try to realize itself in man as truth and reality, but also as goodness. This goodness consists, at least in part, in trying to attain truth and reality and beauty. In a way, these obligations are based on our social nature, for we would not be real, or capable of understanding, except that we are social. But they transcend the social; just as social duties may be inconsistent with each other, so these universal obligations may be inconsistent with social obligations. We may regard this inconsistency as placing the whole matter on the level of Appearance (in Bradley's later terminology) and so driving us to something still farther off in order to effect a reconciliation. What we are driven to, Bradley says, is religion. In religion, man's actual social self and his ideal universal self are somehow reconciled in the acceptance of God, and in the way in which we are at one and the same time set apart from God and yet united with Him.

In later years, when Bradley had elaborated a complete metaphysical system, religion, too, seemed insufficient and even God was subordinated to the Absolute. But this is just a higher dialectical stage; the principles of the solution are the same. In practical terms, however, the problem of conflicting duties is not resolved however much it seems, verbally, to disappear. A man must act, and any attempt to reconcile the opposition between his duties as a social being and his duties as an ideal, or a natural being, by the invocation of religion only raises another problem: should one fulfill his religious duties even where they conflict with other duties? Bradley's emphasis on the social nature of man was a badly needed antidote to the extreme individualism of the empiricist tradition. Carried too far, the antidote is worse than the disease for it denies the individuality of man and leads to his total subordination to the State. Bradley was too honest to deny all other aspects of man's nature but the social one; he was too well aware of the power of the individual mind for any such folly.

But Bradley's solution of man's dualism is not sufficient to permit criticism of the conventionally moral and of human institutions. The problem remains of doing justice to the natural and genetic aspects of man, on the one hand, and his social aspect, on the other. Then the philosopher, on the basis of an adequate social theory, must formulate criteria in terms of which we can make particular judgments of value, so that we can adjust society to changing conditions, preserving what is valuable and eliminating what is not valuable.

IV

For a time, Bradley and the other British Idealists constituted a new orthodoxy, as did their counterparts in America. Then empiricism and naturalism returned, in a more sophisticated version, and became, at the least, an equally accepted alternative. A good deal of the new sophistication of the empiricists was a result of idealist criticism. Mind was no longer regarded as passive, or initially "blank," nor were social influences on mind and behavior neglected. But reading Bradley today is not to be justified only by his historical importance, or the qualities of his prose, though they are excellent justifications.

Bradley carried a specific set of beliefs about as far as they could go; he thought through the problems he set himself, with stubbornness and honesty. If we find some of his arguments to be purely verbal, even when he regards them as something more, we cannot thereby impugn his integrity. If we find his dialectic sometimes confusing or equivocal, we cannot therefore deprecate his brilliance. Our assumptions and our criteria may be different, and we can refuse to accept his conclusions. But we should be willing to learn from him and to formulate his best insights in our own terms.

It is easy to be misled by the articulateness of contemporary naturalists into the belief that their doctrines are more widely understood and accepted than they actually are. Bradley's presuppositions are still current, even when they are called by a variety of names, and one can find them in political theories, in the writings of some gestalt psychologists, in the social philosophizing of some anthropologists, in educational philosophy, institutional theory, and so on. The basic difference between Bradley and most of those who share his assumptions is that Bradley carried the argument through. If we are prepared to follow him, to see where the beliefs lead when they are treated with great intelligence and care, we can understand better the full implications of much contemporary thinking.

RALPH G. ROSS

New York University
November, 1950

Ethical Studies

(Selected Essays)

NOTE ON THE EDITION

The material selected and reprinted here is of two kinds: the most important of Bradley's polemics (against the Utilitarians and against the Kantians); and the chief line of constructive theory in the *Ethical Studies*. It is essentially on the following Essays that Bradley's reputation as an original moralist must rest.

The Essays have been reprinted in their entirety, including his Notes and footnotes. Spelling and punctuation have been revised to conform to current American usage. Since the author makes repeated references to several of the Essays which are not included in this edition, we here for the convenience of the reader give the table of contents of the complete edition.

R. G. R.

WHY SHOULD I BE MORAL?

W HY should I be moral?[1] The question is natural, and yet seems strange. It appears to be one we ought to ask, and yet we feel, when we ask it, that we are wholly removed from the moral point of view.

To ask the question Why? is rational; for reason teaches us to do nothing blindly, nothing without end or aim. She teaches us that what is good must be good for something, and that what is good for nothing is not good at all. And so we take it as certain that there is an end on one side, means on the other; and that only if the end is good, and the means conduce to it, have we a right to say the means are good. It is rational, then, always to inquire, Why should I do it?

But here the question seems strange. For morality (and she too is reason) teaches us that, if we look on her only as good for something else, we never in that case have seen her at all. She says that she is an end to be desired for her own sake, and not as a means to something beyond. Degrade her, and she disappears; and to keep her, we must love and not merely use her. And so at the question Why? we are in trouble, for that does assume and does take for granted that virtue in this sense is unreal, and what we believe is false. Both virtue and the asking Why? seem rational, and yet incompatible one with the other; and the better course will be, not forthwith to reject virtue in favor of the question, but rather to inquire concerning the nature of the Why?

[1] Let me observe here that the word "moral" has three meanings, which must be throughout these pages distinguished by the context. (1) Moral is opposed to *non*moral. The moral world, or world of morality, is opposed to the natural world, where morality cannot exist. (2) Within the moral world of moral agents, "moral" is opposed to *im*moral. (3) Again, within the moral world, and the moral part of the moral world, "moral" is further restricted to the *personal* side of the moral life and the moral institutions. It stands for the *inner* relation of this or that will to the universal, not to the whole, outer and inner, realization of morality.

3

Why should I be virtuous? Why should I? Could anything be more modest? Could anything be less assuming? It is not a dogma; it is only a question. And yet a question may contain (perhaps must contain) an assumption more or less hidden; or, in other words, a dogma. Let us see what is assumed in the asking of our question.

In "Why should I be moral?" the "Why should I?" was another way of saying, What good is virtue? or rather, For what is it good? and we saw that in asking, Is virtue good as a means, and how so? we do assume that virtue is not good, except as a means. The dogma at the root of the question is hence clearly either: (1) the general statement that only means are good; or (2) the particular assertion of this in the case of virtue.

To explain: the question For what? Whereto? is either universally applicable, or not so. It holds everywhere, or we mean it to hold only here. Let us suppose, in the first place, that it is meant to hold everywhere.

Then (1) we are taking for granted that nothing is good in itself; that only the means to something else are good; that "good," in a word, = "good for," and good for something else. Such is the general canon by which virtue would have to be measured.

No one perhaps would explicitly put forward such a canon, and yet it may not be waste of time to examine it.

The good is a means: a means is a means to something else, and this is an end. Is the end good? No, if we hold to our general canon, it is not good as an end; the good was always good for something else, and was a means. To be good, the end must be a means, and so on forever in a process which has no limit. If we ask now What is good? we must answer, There is nothing which is *not* good, for there is nothing which may not be regarded as conducing to something outside itself. Everything is relative to something else. And the essence of the good is to exist by virtue of something else and something else forever. Everything *is* something else, is the result which at last we are brought to, if we insist on pressing our canon as universally applicable.

But the above is not needed perhaps; for those who introduced the question Why? did not think of things in general. The good for them was not an infinite process of idle distinction. Their interest is practical, and they do and must understand by the good (which they call a means) some means to an end in itself; which latter they assume and unconsciously fix in whatever is agreeable to themselves. If we said to them, for example: "Virtue is a means, and so is everything besides, and a means to everything else besides. Virtue is a means to pleasure, pain, health, disease, wealth, poverty, and is a good, because a means; and so also with pain, poverty, etc. They are all good, because all are means. Is this what you mean by the question Why?" They would answer No. And they would answer No because something has been taken as an end, and therefore good, and has been assumed dogmatically.

The universal application of the question For what? or Whereto? is, we see, repudiated. The question does not hold good everywhere, and we must now consider, secondly, its particular application to virtue.

(2) Something is here assumed to be the end; and further, this is assumed *not* to be virtue; and thus the question is founded, "Is virtue a means to a given end, which end is the good? Is virtue good? and why? *i.e.*, as conducing to what good is it good?" The dogma A or B or C is a good in itself justifies the inquiry, Is D a means to A, B, or C? And it is the dogmatic character of the question that we wished to point out. Its rationality, put as if universal, is tacitly assumed to end with a certain province; and our answer must be this: *If* your formula will not (on your own admission) apply to everything, what ground have you for supposing it to apply to virtue? "Be virtuous that you may be happy (*i.e.*, pleased)"; then why be happy, and not rather virtuous? "The pleasure of all is an end." *Why* all? "Mine." *Why* mine? Your reply must be that you take it to be so and are prepared to argue on the thesis that something not virtue is the end in itself. And so are we; and we shall try to show that this is erroneous. But even if we fail in that, we have, I hope, made it clear that the question Why should I be moral? rests on the assertion of an end in itself, which is not

morality;[2] and a point of this importance must not be taken for granted.

It is quite true that to ask Why should I be moral? is *ipso facto* to take one view of morality, is to assume that virtue is a means to something not itself. But it is a mistake to suppose that the general asking of Why? affords any presumption in favor of, or against, any one theory. If any theory could stand upon the What for? as a rational formula, which must always hold good and be satisfied, then, to that extent, no doubt it would have an advantage. But we have seen that all doctrines alike must reject the What for? and agree in this rejection, if they agree in nothing else; since they all must have an end which is not a mere means. And if so, is it not foolish to suppose that its giving a reason for virtue is any argument in favor of Hedonism, when for its own end it can give no reason at all? Is it not clear that, if you have any Ethics, you must have an end which is above the Why? in the sense of What for?; and that, if this is so, the question is now, as it was two thousand years ago, Granted that there is an end, *what* is this end? And the asking that question, as reason and history both tell us, is not in itself the presupposing of a Hedonistic answer, or any other answer.

The claim of pleasure to be the end, we are to discuss in another paper. But what is clear at first sight is that to take virtue as mere means to an ulterior end is in direct antagonism to the voice of the moral consciousness.

That consciousness, when unwarped by selfishness and not blinded by sophistry, is convinced that to ask for the Why? is simple immorality; to do good for its own sake is virtue, to do it for some ulterior end or object, not itself good, is never virtue; and never to act but for the sake of an end, other than doing well and right, is the mark of vice. And the theory which sees in virtue, as in money-getting, a means which is mistaken for an end,

[2] "The question itself [Why should I do right?] cannot be put, except in a form which assumes that the Utilitarian answer is the only one which can possibly be given. . . . The words 'Why should I' mean 'What shall I get by,' 'What motive have I for' this or that course of conduct?"—F. STEPHEN, *Liberty, Equality, and Fraternity* (2nd ed., London, 1873), p. 361.

contradicts the voice which proclaims that virtue not only does seem to be, but is, an end in itself.[3]

[3] There are two points which we may notice here. (1) There is a view which says, "Pleasure (or pain) is what moves you to act; therefore, pleasure (or pain) is your motive, and is always the Why? of your actions. You think otherwise by virtue of a psychological illusion." For a consideration of this view we must refer to Essay VII [omitted in this edition]. We may, however, remark in passing, that this view confuses the motive, which is an object before the mind, with the psychical stimulus, which is not an object before the mind and therefore is not a motive nor a Why? in the sense of an end proposed.

(2) There is a view which tries to found moral philosophy on theology, a theology of a somewhat coarse type, consisting mainly in the doctrine of a criminal judge, of superhuman knowledge and power, who has promulgated and administers a criminal code. This may be called the "do it or be d——d" theory of morals, and is advocated or timidly suggested by writers nowadays, not so much (it seems probable) because in most cases they have a strong, or even a weak, belief in it, but because it stops holes in theories which they feel, without some help of the kind, will not hold water. We are not concerned with this opinion as a theological doctrine, and will merely remark that, as such, it appears to us to contain the essence of irreligion; but with respect to morals, we say that, let it be never so true, it contributes nothing to moral philosophy, unless that has to do with the means whereby we are simply to get pleasure or avoid pain. The theory not only confuses morality and religion, but reduces them both to deliberate selfishness. Fear of criminal proceedings in the other world does not tell us what is morally right in this world. It merely gives a selfish motive for obedience to those who believe, and leaves those who do not believe, in all cases with less motive, in some cases with none. I cannot forbear remarking that, so far as my experience goes, where future punishments are firmly believed in, the fear of them has, in most cases, but little influence on the mind. And the facts do not allow us to consider the fear of punishment in this world as the main motive to morality. In most cases there is, properly speaking, *no* ulterior motive. A man is moral because he likes being moral; and he likes it, partly because he has been brought up to the habit of liking it, and partly because he finds it gives him what he wants, while its opposite does not do so. He is not as a rule kept "straight" by the contemplation of evils to be inflicted on him from the outside; and the shame he feels at the bad opinion of others is not a mere external evil, and is not feared simply as such. In short, a man is a human being, something larger than the abstraction of an actual or possible criminal.

Taking our stand then, as we hope, on this common consciousness, what answer can we give when the question Why should I
be moral? — in the sense of What will it advantage me? — is put
to us? Here we shall do well, I think, to avoid all praises of the
pleasantness of virtue. We may believe that it transcends all
possible delights of vice, but it would be well to remember that
we desert a moral point of view, that we degrade and prostitute
virtue, when to those who do not love her for herself we
bring ourselves to recommend her for the sake of her pleasures.
Against the base mechanical βαναυσία, which meets us on all sides,
with its "What is the use" of goodness or beauty or truth? there
is but one fitting answer from the friends of science or art or
religion and virtue, "We do not know and we do not care."

As a direct answer to the question we should not say more;
but, putting ourselves at our questioner's point of view, we may
ask in return, Why should I be immoral? Is it not disadvan-
tageous to be so? We can ask, is your view consistent? Does
it satisfy you and give you what you want? And if you are
satisfied, and so far as you are satisfied, do see whether it is not
because, and so far as, you are false to your theory; so far as you
are living not directly with a view to the pleasant, but with a
view to something else, or with no view at all, but, as you would
call it, without any "reason." We believe that, in your heart, your
end is what ours is, but that about this end you not only are sorely
mistaken, but in your heart you feel and know it; or at least would
do so if you would only reflect. And more than this I think we
ought not to say.

What more are we to say? If a man asserts total skepticism,
you cannot argue with him. You can show that he contradicts
himself; but if he says, "I do not care"—there is an end of it. So,
too, if a man says, "I shall do what I like because I happen to
like it; and as for ends, I recognize none"—you may indeed show
him that his conduct is in fact otherwise; and if he will assert
anything as an end, if he will but say, "I have no end but myself,"
then you may argue with him and try to prove that he is making
a mistake as to the nature of the end he alleges. But if he says,
"I care not whether I am moral or rational, nor how much I con-

tradict myself," then argument ceases. We who have the power believe that what is rational (if it is not yet) at least is to be real, and decline to recognize anything else. For standing on reason we can give, of course, no further reason; but we push our reason against what seems to oppose it, and soon force all to see that moral obligations do not vanish where they cease to be felt or are denied.

Has the question, Why should I be moral? no sense then, and is no positive answer possible? No, the question has no sense at all; it is simply unmeaning unless it is equivalent to, *Is* morality an end in itself; and if so, how and in what way is it an end? Is morality the same as the end for man, so that the two are convertible; or is morality one side or aspect or element of some end which is larger than itself? Is it the whole end from all points of view or is it one view of the whole? Is the artist moral, so far as he is a good artist, or the philosopher moral, so far as he is a good philosopher? Are their art or science and their virtue one thing from one and the same point of view or two different things, or one thing from two points of view?

These are not easy questions to answer, and we cannot discuss them yet. We have taken the reader now so far as he need go, before proceeding to the following essays. What remains is to point out the most general expression for the end in itself, the ultimate practical "why"; and that we find in the word *self-realization*. But what follows is an anticipation of the sequel, which we cannot promise to make intelligible as yet; and the reader who finds difficulties had better go on at once to Essay III ["Pleasure for Pleasure's Sake"].

How can it be proved that self-realization is the end? There is only one way to do that. This is to know what we mean when we say "self" and "real" and "realize" and "end"; and to know that is to have something like a system of metaphysic, and to say it would be to exhibit that system. Instead of remarking then that we lack space to develop our views, let us frankly confess that, properly speaking, we have no such views to develop, and therefore we cannot *prove* our thesis. All that we can do is partially to explain it, and try to render it plausible. It is a formula which our succeeding Essays will in some way fill up, and which here we shall attempt to recommend to the reader beforehand.

An objection will occur at once. "There surely are ends," it will be said, "which are not myself, which fall outside my activity, and which, nevertheless, I do realize and think I ought to realize." We must try to show that the objection rests upon a misunderstanding; and, as a statement of fact, brings with it insuperable difficulties.

Let us first go to the moral consciousness and see what that tells us about its end.

Morality implies an end in itself — we take that for granted. Something is to be done, a good is to be realized. But that result is, by itself, not morality; morality differs from art in that it cannot make the act a *mere* means to the result. Yet there is a means. There is not only something to be done, but something to be done by me — *I* must do the act, must realize the end. Morality implies both the something to be done and the doing of it by me; and if you consider them as end and means, you cannot separate the end and the means. If you chose to change the position of end and means and say my doing is the end and the "to be done" is the means, you would not violate the moral consciousness; for the truth is that means and end are not applicable here. The act for me means my act, and there is no end beyond the act. This we see in the belief that failure may be equivalent morally to success — in the saying that there is nothing good except a good will. In short, for morality the end implies the act, and the act implies self-realization. This, if it were doubtful, would be shown (we may remark in passing) by the feeling of pleasure which attends the putting forth of the act. For if pleasure be the feeling of self and accompany the act, this indicates that the putting forth of the act is also the putting forth of the self.

But we must not lay too much stress on the moral consciousness, for we shall be reminded, perhaps, that not only can it be, but, like the miser's consciousness, it frequently has been explained; and that both states of mind are illusions generated on one and the same principle.

Let us then dismiss the moral consciousness and not trouble ourselves about what we think we ought to do; let us try to show that what we do is, perfectly or imperfectly, to realize ourselves, and that we cannot possibly do anything else; that all we can realize is (accident apart) our ends, or the objects we desire; and that all we can desire is, in a word, self.

This, we think, will be readily admitted by our main psychological party. What we wish to avoid is that it should be admitted in a form which makes it unmeaning; and of this there is perhaps some danger. We do not want the reader to say, "Oh yes, of course, relativity of knowledge — everything is a state of consciousness," and so dismiss the question. If the reader believes that a steam engine, after it is made, is nothing[4] but a state of the mind of the person or persons who have made it, or who are looking at it, we do not hold what we feel tempted to call such a silly doctrine; and would point out to those who do hold it that, at all events, the engine is a very different state of mind after it is made to what it was before.

Again, we do not want the reader to say, "Certainly, every object or end which I propose to myself is, as such, a mere state of my mind—it is a thought in my head, or a state of me; and so, when it becomes real, I become real"; because, though it is very true that my thought, as my thought, cannot exist apart from me thinking it, and therefore my proposed end must, as such, be a

---

[4] We may remark that the ordinary "philosophical" person who talks about "relativity," really does not seem to know what he is saying. He will tell you that "all" (or "all we know and can know"—there is no practical difference between that and "all") is relative to consciousness—not giving you to understand that he means thereby any consciousness beside his own, and ready, I should imagine, with his grin at the notion of a mind which is anything more than the mind of this or that man; and then, it may be a few pages further on or further back, will talk to you of the state of the earth before man existed on it. But we wish to know what in the world it all means, and would suggest, as a method of clearing the matter, the two questions—(1) Is my consciousness something that goes and is beyond myself; and if so, in what sense? and (2) Had I a father? What do I mean by that, and how do I reconcile my assertion of it with my answer to question (1)?

state of me,[5] yet this is not what we are driving at. All my ends are my thoughts, but all my thoughts are not my ends; and if what we meant by self-realization was that I have in my head the idea of any future external event, then I should realize myself practically when I see that the engine is going to run off the line, and it does so.

A desired object (as desired) is a thought, and my thought, but it is something more and that something more is, in short, that it is desired by me. And we ought by right, before we go further, to exhibit a theory of desire; but, if we could do that, we could not stop to do it. However, we say with confidence that, in desire, what is desired must in all cases be self.

If we could accept the theory that the end or motive is always the idea of a pleasure (or pain) of our own, which is associated with the object presented, and which is that in the object which moves us, and the only thing which does move us, then from such a view it would follow at once that all we can aim at is a state of ourselves.

We cannot, however, accept the theory, since we believe it both to ignore and to be contrary to facts (see Essay VII); but, though we do not admit that the motive is always, or in most cases, the idea of a state of our feeling self, yet we think it is clear that nothing moves unless it be desired and that what is desired is ourself. For all objects or ends have been associated with our satisfaction, or (more correctly) have been felt in and as ourselves, or we have felt ourselves therein; and the only reason why they move us now is that when they are presented to our minds as motives we do now feel ourselves asserted or affirmed in them. The essence of desire for an object would thus be the feeling of our affirmation in the idea of something not ourself, felt against the feeling of ourself as, without the object, void and negated; and it is the tension of this relation which produces motion. If so, then nothing is desired except that which is identified with ourselves, and we can aim at nothing except so far as we aim at ourselves in it.

[5] Let me remark in passing that it does not follow from this that it is nothing but a state of me, as this or that man.

But passing by the above, which we cannot here expound and which we lay no stress on, we think that the reader will probably go with us so far as this, that in desire what we want, so far as we want it, is ourselves in some form, or is some state of ourselves; and that our wanting anything else would be psychologically inexplicable.

Let us take this for granted then; but is this what we mean by self-realization? Is the conclusion that, in trying to realize, we try to realize some state of ourself, all that we are driving at? No, the self we try to realize is for us a whole, it is not a mere collection of states. (See more in Essay III.)

If we may presuppose in the reader a belief in the doctrine that what is wanted is a state of self, we wish, standing upon that, to urge further that the whole self is present in its states, and that therefore the whole self is the object aimed at; and this is what we mean by self-realization. If a state of self is what is desired, can you, we wish to ask, have states of self which are states of nothing (compare Essay I); can you possibly succeed in regarding the self as a collection or stream or train or series or aggregate? If you cannot think of it as a mere one, can you on the other hand think of it as a mere many, as mere ones; or are you not driven, whether you wish it or not, to regard it as a one in many, or a many in one? Are we not forced to look on the self as a whole which is not merely the sum of its parts, nor yet some other particular beside them? And must we not say that to realize self is always to realize a whole, and that the question in morals is to find the true whole, realizing which will practically realize the true self?

This is the question which to the end of this volume we shall find ourselves engaged on. For the present, turning our attention away from it in this form, and contenting ourselves with the proposition that to realize is to realize self, let us now, apart from questions of psychology or metaphysics, see what ends they are, in fact, which living men do propose to themselves and whether these do not take the form of a whole.

Upon this point there is no need, I think, to dwell at any

length; for it seems clear that if we ask ourselves what it is we should most wish for, we find some general wish which would include and imply our particular wishes. And if we turn to life we see that no man has disconnected particular ends; he looks beyond the moment, beyond this or that circumstance or position; his ends are subordinated to wider ends; each situation is seen (consciously or unconsciously) as part of a broader situation, and in this or that act he is aiming at and realizing some larger whole which is not real in any particular act as such, and yet is realized in the body of acts which carry it out. We need not stop here because the existence of larger ends, which embrace smaller ends, cannot be doubted; and so far we may say that the self we realize is identified with wholes, or that the ideas of the states of self we realize are associated with ideas that stand for wholes.

But is it also true that these larger wholes are included in one whole? I think that it is. I am not forgetting that we act, as a rule, not *from* principle or with the principle before us, and I wish the reader not to forget that the principle may be there and may be our basis or our goal, without our knowing anything about it. And here, of course, I am not saying that it has occurred to every one to ask himself whether he aims at a whole, and what that is; because considerable reflection is required for this, and the amount need not have been reached. Nor again am I saying that every man's actions are consistent, that he does not wander from his end, and that he has not particular ends which will not come under his main end. Nor further do I assert that the life of every man does form a whole; that in some men there are not coordinated ends which are incompatible and incapable of subordination into a system.[6] What I am saying is that if the life of the normal man be inspected and the ends he has in view (as exhibited in his acts) be considered, they will, roughly speaking, be embraced in one main end or whole of ends. It has been said that "every man has a different notion of happiness," but this is scarcely correct unless mere detail be referred to. Certainly,

[6] The unhappiness of such lives in general, however, points to the fact that the real end is a whole. Dissatisfaction rises from the knowing or feeling that the self is not realized, and not realized because not realized as a system.

however, every man has *a* notion of happiness, and *his* notion, though he may not quite know what it is. Most men have a life which they live and with which they are tolerably satisfied, and that life, when examined, is seen to be fairly systematic; it is seen to be a sphere including spheres, the lower spheres subordinating to themselves and qualifying particular actions, and themselves subordinated to and qualified by the whole. And most men have more or less of an ideal of life — a notion of perfect happiness which is never quite attained in real life; and if you take (not of course any one, but) the normal decent and serious man, when he has been long enough in the world to know what he wants, you will find that his notion of perfect happiness or ideal life is not something straggling, as it were, and discontinuous, but is brought before the mind as an unity, and, if imagined more in detail, is a system where particulars subserve one whole.

Without further dwelling on this I will ask the reader to reflect whether the ends, proposed to themselves by ordinary persons, are not wholes, and are not in the end members in a larger whole; and if that be so, whether, since it is so, and since all we can want must (as before stated) be ourselves, we must not now say that we aim not only at the realization of self, but of self as a whole, seeing that there is a general object of desire with which self is identified, or (on another view) with the idea of which the idea of our pleasure is associated.

Up to the present we have been trying to point out that what we aim at is self, and self as a whole; in other words, that self as a whole is in the end the content of our wills. It will still further, perhaps, tend to clear the matter if we refer to the form of the will — not, of course, suggesting that the form is anything real apart from the content.

On this head we are obliged to restrict ourselves to the assertion of what we believe to be fact. We remarked in our last Essay [I] that, in saying "I will this or that," we really mean something. In saying it we do not mean (at least, not as a rule) to distinguish a self that wills from a self that does not will; but what we do mean is to distinguish the self, as will in general, from this or that object of desire, and, at the same time, to identify the two; to say, this or that is willed, or the will has uttered itself in this or that. The will is looked on as a whole, and there are two sides or factors to that whole. Let us consider an act of will and, that we may see more clearly, let us take a deliberate volitional choice. We have conflicting desires, say A and B; we feel two tensions, two drawings (so to speak), but we cannot actually affirm ourselves in both. Action does not follow, and we reflect on the two objects of desire and we are aware that we are reflecting on them, or (if our language allowed us to say it) over them. But we do not merely stand looking on till, so to speak, we find we are gone in one direction, have closed with A or B. For we are aware besides of ourselves, not simply as something theoretically above A and B, but as something also practically above them, as a concentration which is not one or the other, but which is the possibility of either, which is the inner side indifferently of an act which should realize A, or one which should realize B, and hence, which is neither, and yet is superior to both. In short, we do not simply feel ourselves in A and B, but have distinguished ourselves from both, as what is above both. This is one factor in volition and it is hard to find any name better for it than that of the universal factor, or side, or moment.[7] We need say much less about the second factor. In order to will, we must will something; the universal side by itself is not will at all. To will we must identify ourselves with this, that, or the other; and here we have the particular side, and

[7] As we saw in our last Essay [I], there are two dangers to avoid here, in the shape of two one-sided views, Scylla and Charybdis. The first is the ignoring of the universal side altogether, even as an element; the second is the assertion of it as more than an element, as by itself will. Against this second it is necessary to insist that the will is what it wills, that to will you must will something, and that you cannot will the mere form of the will; further, that the mere formal freedom of choice not only, if it were real, would *not* be true freedom, but that, in addition, it is a metaphysical fiction; that the universal is real only as one side of the whole and takes its character from the whole; and that, in the most deliberate and would-be formal volition, the self that is abstracted and stands above the particulars is the abstraction not only from the particular desire or desires before the mind, but also from the whole self, the self which embodies all past acts, and that *the abstraction is determined by that from which it is abstracted,* no less than itself is a moment in the determination of the concrete act.

the second factor in volition. Thirdly, the volition as a whole (and first, as a whole, is it volition) is the identity of both these factors, and the projection or carrying of it out into external existence; the realization both of the particular side, the this or that to be done, and the realization of the inner side of self in the doing of it, with a realization of self in both, as is proclaimed by the feeling of pleasure. This unity of the two factors we may call the individual whole, or again the concrete universal; and, although we are seldom conscious of the distinct factors, yet every act of will will be seen, when analyzed, to be a whole of this kind, and so to realize what is always the nature of the will.

But to what end have we made this statement? Our object has been to draw the attention of the reader to the fact that not only what is willed by men, the end they set before themselves, is a whole, but also that the will itself, looked at apart from any particular object or content, is a similar whole; or, to put it in its proper order, the self is realized in a whole of ends because it is a whole, and because it is not satisfied till it has found itself, till content be adequate to form, and that content be realized; and this is what we mean by practical self-realization.

"Realize yourself," "realize yourself as a whole," is the result of the foregoing. The reader, I fear, may be wearied already by these prefatory remarks, but it will be better in the end if we delay yet longer. All we know at present is that we are to realize self as *a* whole; but as to *what* whole it is, we know nothing and must further consider.

The end we desire (to repeat it) is the finding and possessing ourselves as a whole. We aim at this both in theory and practice. What we want in theory is to understand the object; we want neither to remove nor alter the world of sensuous fact, but we want to get at the truth of it. The whole of science takes it for granted that the "not-ourself" is really intelligible; it stands and falls with this assumption. So long as our theory strikes on the mind as strange and alien, so long do we say we have not found truth; we feel the impulse to go beyond and beyond, we alter and alter our views till we see them as a consistent whole.

There we rest because then we have found the nature of our own mind and the truth of facts in one. And in practice again, with a difference, we have the same want. Here our aim is not, leaving the given as it is, to find the truth of it; but here we want to force the sensuous fact to correspond to the truth of ourselves. We say, "My sensuous existence is thus, but I truly am not thus; I am different." On the one hand, as a matter of fact, I and my existing world are discrepant; on the other hand, the instinct of my nature tells me that the world is mine. On that impulse I act, I alter and alter the sensuous facts till I find in them nothing but myself carried out. Then I possess my world, and I do not possess it until I find my will in it; and I do not find that until what I have is a harmony or a whole in system.

Both in theory and practice my end is to realize myself as a whole. But is this all? Is a *consistent* view all that we want in theory? Is a *harmonious* life all that we want in practice? Certainly not. A doctrine must not only hold together, but it must hold the facts together as well. We cannot rest in it simply because it does not contradict itself. The theory must take in the facts, and an ultimate theory must take in all the facts. So again in practice. It is no human ideal to lead "the life of an oyster." We have no right first to find out just what we happen to be and to have, and then to contract our wants to that limit. We cannot do it if we would, and morality calls to us that, if we try to do it, we are false to ourselves. Against the sensuous facts around us and within us we must forever attempt to widen our empire; we must at least try to go forward or we shall certainly be driven back.

So self-realization means more than the mere assertion of the self as a whole.[8] And here we may refer to two principles which Kant put forward under the names of "Homogeneity" and "Specification." Not troubling ourselves with our relation to Kant, we may say that the ideal is neither to be perfectly homogeneous nor simply to be specified to the last degree, but rather to combine

---

[8] I leave out of sight the important question whether any partial whole *can* be self-consistent. If (which seems the better view) this cannot be, we shall not need to say "Systematize *and* widen," but the second will be implied in the first.

both these elements. Our true being is not the extreme of unity, nor of diversity, but the perfect identity of both. And "Realize yourself" does not mean merely "Be a whole," but "Be an *infinite* whole."

At this word I am afraid the reader who has not yet despaired of us will come to a stop and refuse to enter into the region of nonsense. But why should it be nonsense? When the poet and the preacher tell us the mind is infinite, most of us feel that it is so; and has our science really come to this that the beliefs which answer to our highest feelings must be theoretical absurdities? Should not the philosophy which tells us such a thing be very sure of the ground it goes upon? But if the reader will follow me I think I can show him that the mere finitude of the mind is a more difficult thesis to support than its infinity.

It would be well if I could ask the reader to tell me what he means by "finite." As that cannot be I must say that finite is limited or ended. To be finite is to be some one among others, some one which is *not* others. One finite ends where the other finite begins; it is bounded from the outside, and cannot go beyond itself without becoming something else, and thereby perishing.[9]

"The mind," we are told, "is finite; and the reason why we say it is finite is that we know it is finite. The mind knows that itself is finite." This is the doctrine we have to oppose.

We answer, The mind is *not* finite just because it knows it *is* finite. "The knowledge of the limit suppresses the limit." It is a flagrant self-contradiction that the finite should know its own finitude; and it is not hard to make this plain.

Finite means limited from the outside and by the outside. The finite is to know itself as this, or not as finite. If its knowledge ceases to fall wholly within itself, then so far it is not finite. It knows that it is limited from the outside and by the outside, and that means it knows the outside. But if so, then it is so far not finite. If its whole being fell within itself, then in knowing

[9] We have to dwell on the inherent contradiction of the finite. Its being is to fall wholly within itself; and yet, so far as it is finite, so far is it determined wholly by the outside.

itself it could not know that there was anything outside itself. It does do the latter; hence the former supposition is false.

Imagine a man shut up in a room, who said to us, "My faculties are entirely confined to the *inside* of this room. The limit of the room is the limit of my mind and so I can have no knowledge whatever of the outside"; should we not answer, "My dear sir, you contradict yourself. If it were as you say, you could not know of an outside, and so, by consequence, not of an inside, as such. You should be in earnest and go through with your doctrine of 'relativity.' "

To the above simple argument I fear we may not have done justice. However that be, I know of no answer to it; and until we find one, we must say that it is not true that the mind is finite.

If I am to realize myself it must be as infinite; and now the question is, What does infinite mean? and it will be better to say first what it does not mean. There are two wrong views on the subject, which we will take one at a time.

(1) Infinite is not-finite, and that means "end-less." What does endless mean? Not the mere negation of end, because a mere negation is nothing at all, and infinite would thus = O. The endless is something positive; it means a positive quantity which has no end. Any given number of units is finite, but a series of units which is produced indefinitely is infinite. This is the sense of infinite which is in most common use, and which, we shall see, is what Hedonism believes in. It is however clear that this infinite is a perpetual self-contradiction and, so far as it is real, is only finite. Any real quantity has ends beyond which it does not go. "Increase the quantity" merely says, "Put the end further off"; but in saying that, it does say "Put the end." "Increase the quantity forever" means, "Have forever a finite quantity, and forever say that it is not finite." In other words, "Remove the end" does imply, by that very removal and the production of the series, the making of a fresh end; so that we still have a finite quantity. Here, so far as the infinite exists, it is finite; so far as it is told to exist, it is told again to be nothing but finite.

(2) Or, secondly, the infinite is *not* the finite, no longer in the sense of being more in quantity, but in the sense of being some-

thing else which is different in quality. The infinite is not in the world of limited things; it exists in a sphere of its own. The mind (*e. g.*) is something *beside* the aggregate of its states. God is something beside the things of this world. This is the infinite believed in by abstract Duty. But here once more, against its will, infinite comes to mean merely finite. The infinite is a something over against, beside, and outside the finite; and hence is itself also finite, because limited by something else.

In neither of these two senses is the mind infinite. What then is the true sense of infinite? As before, it is the negation of the finite; it is not-finite. But, unlike both the false infinites, it does not leave the finite as it is. It neither, with (1), says "the finite *is to be* not-finite," nor, with (2), tries to get rid of it by doubling it. It does really negate the finite so that the finite disappears, not by having a negative set over against it, but by being taken up into a higher unity in which, becoming an element, it ceases to have its original character and is both suppressed and preserved. The infinite is thus "the unity of the finite and infinite." The finite was determined from the outside, so that everywhere to characterize and distinguish it was in fact to divide it. Wherever you defined anything you were at once carried beyond to something else and something else, and this because the negative, required for distinction, was an outside other. In the infinite you can distinguish without dividing; for this is an unity holding within itself subordinated factors which are negative of, and so distinguishable from, each other; while at the same time the whole is so present in each that each has its own being in its opposite, and depends on that relation for its own life. The negative is also its affirmation. Thus the infinite has a distinction, and so a negation, in itself, but is distinct from and negated by nothing but itself. Far from being one something which is *not* another something, it is a whole in which both one and the other are mere elements. This whole is hence "relative" utterly and through and through, but the relation does not fall outside it; the relatives are moments in which it is the relation of itself to itself, and so is above the relation, and is absolute reality. The finite is relative to something *else;* the infinite is *self*-related.

It is this sort of infinite which the mind is. The simplest symbol of it is the circle, the line which returns into itself, not the straight line produced indefinitely; and the readiest way to find it is to consider the satisfaction of desire. There we have myself and its opposite, and the return from the opposite, the finding in the other nothing but self. And here it would be well to recall what we said above on the form of the will.

If the reader to whom this account of the infinite is new has found it in any way intelligible, I think he will see that there is some sense in it when we say, "Realize yourself as an infinite whole"; or, in other words, "Be specified in yourself, but not specified by anything foreign to yourself."

But the objection comes: "Morality tells us to progress; it tells us we are not concluded in ourselves nor perfect, but that there exists a not-ourself which never does wholly become ourself. And apart from morality, it is obvious that I and you, this man and the other man, are finite beings. We are not one another; more or less we must limit each other's sphere; I am what I am more or less by external relations, and I do not fall wholly within myself. Thus I am to be infinite, to have no limit from the outside; and yet I am one among others, and therefore am finite. It is all very well to tell me that in me there is infinity, the perfect identity of subject and object — that I may be willing perhaps to believe, but nonetheless I am finite."

We admit the full force of the objection. I *am* finite; I am both infinite *and* finite and that is why my moral life is a perpetual progress. I must progress because I have an other which is to be, and yet never quite is, myself; and so, as I am, am in a state of contradiction.

It is not that I wish to increase the mere quantity of my true self. It is that I wish to be nothing *but* my true self, to be rid of all external relations, to bring them all within me, and so to fall wholly within myself.

I am to be perfectly homogeneous; but I cannot be unless fully specified, and the question is, How can I be extended so as to take in my external relations? Goethe has said, "Be a whole *or* join a whole,"[10] but to that we must answer, "You cannot be a whole, *unless* you join a whole."

The difficulty is: being limited and so not a whole, how extend myself so as to be a whole? The answer is, be a member in a whole. Here your private self, your finitude, ceases as such to exist; it becomes the function of an organism. You must be, not a mere piece of, but a member in, a whole, and as this must know and will yourself.

The whole to which you belong specifies itself in the detail of its functions, and yet remains homogeneous. It lives not many lives but one life, and yet cannot live except in its many members. Just so, each one of the members is alive, but not apart from the whole which lives in it. The organism is homogeneous because it is specified, and specified because it is homogeneous.

"But," it will be said, "what is that to me? I remain one member, and I am not other members. The more perfect the organism, the more is it specified, and so much the intenser becomes its homogeneity. But its 'more' means my 'less.' The unity falls in the whole and so outside me; and the greater specification of the whole means the making me more special, more narrowed and limited, and less developed within myself."

We answer that this leaves out of sight a fact quite palpable and of enormous significance, viz., that in the moral organism the members are aware of themselves, and aware of themselves as members. I do not know myself as mere this, against something else which is not myself. The relations of the others to me are not mere external relations. I know myself as a member; that means I am aware of my own function; but it means also that I am aware of the whole as specifying itself in me. The will of the whole knowingly wills itself in me; the will of the whole is the will of the members, and so, in willing my own function, I do know that the others will themselves in me. I do know again that I will myself in the others, and in them find my will once more as

---

[10] "Immer strebe zum Ganzen, und kannst du selber kein Ganzes Werden, als dienendes Glied schliess' an ein Ganzes dich an."
                                        —*Vier Jahreszeiten,* 45.

not mine, and yet as mine. It is false that the homogeneity falls outside me; it is not only in me, but for me too; and apart from my life in it, my knowledge of it, and devotion to it, I am not myself. When it goes out my heart goes out with it, where it triumphs I rejoice, where it is maimed I suffer; separate me from the love of it and I perish. (See further, Essay V.)

No doubt the distinction of separate selves remains, but the point is this. In morality the existence of my mere private self, as such, is something which ought not to be, and which, so far as I am moral, has already ceased. I am morally realized, not until my personal self has utterly ceased to be my exclusive self, is no more a will which is outside others' wills, but finds in the world of others nothing but self.

"Realize yourself as an infinite whole" means "Realize your-self as the self-conscious member of an infinite whole, by realizing that whole in yourself." When that whole is truly infinite, and when your personal will is wholly made one with it, then you also have reached the extreme of homogeneity and specification in one, and have attained a perfect self-realization.

The foregoing will, we hope, become clear to the reader of this volume. He must consider what has been said so far as the text, which the sequel is to illustrate and work out in detail. Meanwhile, our aim has been to put forward the formula of self-realization and in some measure to explain it. The following Essays will furnish, we hope, something like a commentary and justification. We shall see that the self to be realized is not the self as a collection of particulars, is not the universal as all the states of a certain feeling; and that it is not again an abstract universal, as the form of duty; that neither are in harmony with life, with the moral consciousness, or with themselves; that when the self is identified with, and wills, and realizes a concrete universal, a real totality, then first does it find itself, is satisfied, self-deter-mined, and free—"the free will that wills itself as the free will."

Let us resume, then, the results of the present Essay. We have attempted to show (1) that the formula of "what for?" must be rejected by every ethical doctrine as not universally valid; and that hence no one theory can gain the smallest advantage (except over the foolish) by putting it forward; that now for us (as it was for Hellas) the main question is, There being some end, what is that end? And (2), with which second part, if it fall, the first need not fall, we have endeavored briefly to point out that the final end with which morality is identified, or under which it is included, can be expressed not otherwise than by self-realization.

NOTE

Perhaps the following remarks, though partly repetition of the above, may be of service.

There being an end, that end is realization, at all events; it is something to be reached, otherwise not an end.

And it implies self-realization, because it is to be reached by me. By my action I am to carry it out; in making it real my will is realized, and my will is myself. Hence there is self-realization in all action; witness the feeling of pleasure.

"Yes," it will be said, "but that does not show there is nothing but self-realization. The content of the act is not the self but may be something else, and this something else may be the end. The content is the end."

This is very easy to say but it overlooks the psychological difficulties. How is it possible to will what is not one's self, how can one desire a foreign object? What we desire must be in our minds; we must think of it; and besides, we must be related to it in a particular way. If it is to be the end, we must feel ourselves one with it, and in it; and how can we do that if it does not belong to us and has not been made part of us? To say "thoughts of what is and is to be exist in you, are in your head, and then you carry them out, and that is action" is futile; because these thoughts, if desired, are not merely *in* me, they are felt to be mine, ideally to be myself, and, when they are carried out, that therefore is self-realization.

Or shall we be told that "to talk of carrying out is nonsense. In action we produce changes in things and in ourselves, answering to thoughts; things resemble thoughts, but, strictly speaking, thought is not realized, because that is unmeaning"? If we hold to this, however, we are met by the impossibility then of accounting for thought and action as ordinarily viewed; we should know not the real, but something like the real, and should do not what we mean, intend, have in our minds, but only something like it. But this, unfortunately, is not action. If I do not what I will, but only something like it, then, strictly speaking, so far it is not my act and would not be imputed to me. An act supposes the content on each side to be the same, with a difference, or, under a difference, to be the same. It does suppose that what was in the mind is carried out; and, unless you think that something can be in the self and carried out by the self, without being of the nature of the self (and you would find the difficulties of such a view insuperable), then you must say that volition is self-realization.

But doubtless there are many persons who, not raising metaphysical or psychological questions but standing merely on facts, would say, "Theory apart, surely when I act I do realize more than myself. I quite see that I may not do so; but when I devote myself to a cause, and at my own expense help to carry it out, how then am I realizing only myself?"

The difficulty no doubt is very serious and we cannot pretend here to go to the bottom of it. But we may point out that it arises from a preconception as to the self (i. e., the identification of it with the particular self) which cannot be defended. It is clear that, on the one side, selves do exclude one another. I am not you, you are not he; and, resting on this notion of exclusiveness, we go on to look at the self as a repellent point, or, as we call it, a mere individual. But, apart from metaphysics, facts soon compel us to see that this is not a reality, but an abstraction of our minds. For, without troubling ourselves about the relation of one person to others, as soon as we imagine this mere "individual" acting, we see he must bring forth something, and, to do that, must have something in him, must have a content; and, if so, is not any longer a bare point which we now perceive to be a mere form. Hence we now try to give him a content which falls wholly within himself and is not common to him with others, and, finding it impossible to account for facts on this supposition, suddenly we turn round and fly to the other extreme, and now suppose him to realize the sheer suppression of himself; not seeing that now we have abjured our premises without having refuted them, and are face to face with the psychological difficulty of how a man is to bring out of himself what was not in himself and part of himself, and with the facts which testify that action without interest is a fiction.

But if from a better metaphysic, or attention to facts, we are willing to give up those metaphysical preconceptions we took for fact and now see to be futile, then we may also see that, though certainly one person cannot be, "like Cerberus, three gentlemen at once," yet that, beside being thus exclusive, nonetheless in respect of their content (and that makes them what they are) persons are not thus exclusive; that I am what I will and will what I am, that the content qualifies me, and that there is no reason in the world why that content should be confined to the "this me." In the case of a social being this is impossible; and to point out any human being in whom his exclusive self is the whole content of his will, is out of the question. But, if so, where is the difficulty of my object being one and the same with the object of other people; so that, having filled the form of my personality with a life not merely mine, I have at heart, and have identified with and made one with myself, objective interests, things that are to be, and in and with the existence of which I am not to satisfy my mere private self; so that, as I neither will nor can separate myself from what makes me myself, in realizing them I realize myself, and can do so only by realizing them? (We shall come on this again — see especially Essay VII.)

Well then, just as we must accept the teaching that "all is relative to self," but supplement and correct it with the teaching that "myself also is relative"; so we must accept the teaching of the selfish theory that I can will myself only, but correct it by the addition "and yet the self which is myself, which is mine, is not merely me." Hence that all willing is self-realization is seen not to be in collision with morality.

To conclude — If I am asked why I am to be moral I can say

no more than this, that what I cannot doubt is my own being now, and that since in that being is involved a self, which is to be here and now, and yet in this here and now is not, I therefore cannot doubt that there is an end which I am to make real; and morality, if not equivalent to, is at all events included in this making real of myself.

If it is absurd to ask for the further reason of my knowing and willing my own existence, then it is equally absurd to ask for the further reason of what is involved therein. The only rational question here is not Why? but What? What is the self that I know and will? What is its true nature, and what is implied therein? What is the self that I am to make actual, and how is the principle present, living, and incarnate in its particular modes of realization?

PLEASURE FOR PLEASURE'S SAKE

IT is an old story, a theme too worn for the turning of sentences, and yet too living a moral not to find every day a new point and to break a fresh heart, that our lives are wasted in the pursuit of the impalpable, the search for the impossible and the unmeaning. Neither today nor yesterday, but throughout the whole life of the race, the complaint has gone forth that all is vanity; that the ends for which we live and we die are "mere ideas," illusions begotten on the brain by the wish of the heart— poor phrases that stir the blood, until experience or reflection for a little, and death for all time, bring with it disenchantment and quiet. Duty for duty's sake, life for an end beyond sense, honor, and beauty, and love for the invisible—all these are first felt, and then seen to be dream and shadow and unreal vision. And our cry and our desire is for something that will satisfy us, something that we know and do not only think, something that is real and solid, that we can lay hold of and be sure of and that will not change in our hands. We have said good-by to our transcendent longings, we have bidden a sad but an eternal farewell to the hopes of our own and of the world's too credulous youth; we have parted forever from our early loves, from our fancies and aspirations beyond the human. We seek for the tangible and we find it in this world; for the knowledge which can never deceive, and that is the certainty of our own well-being; we seek for the palpable, and we feel it; for the end which will satisfy us as men, and we find it, in a word, in happiness.

Happiness! Is that climax, or pathos, or cruel irony? Happiness is the end? Yes, happiness is the end which indeed we all reach after; for what more can we wish than that all should be well with us—that our wants should be filled and the desire of our hearts be gratified? And happiness cannot escape us, we must know it when we find it? Oh yes, it would be strange indeed to come to such a consummation and never to know it. And happiness is real and palpable, and we can find it by seeking

29

it? Alas! the one question which no one can answer is, What is happiness? — which everyone in the end can answer is, what happiness is not. It has been called by every name among men, and has been sought on the heights and in the depths; it has been wooed in all the shapes on earth and in heaven, and what man has won it? Its name is a proverb for the visionary object of a universal and a fruitless search; of all the delusions which make a sport of our lives it is not one, but is one common title which covers and includes them all, which shows behind each in turn, but to vanish and appear behind another. The man who says that happiness is his mark, aims at nothing apart from the ends of others. He seeks the illusory goal of all men; and he differs from the rest that are and have been not at all, or only in his assertion that happiness is to be found by seeking it.

"But happiness," will be the reply, "is vague because it has been made so — is impalpable because projected beyond the solid world into the region of cloud and fiction—is visionary because diverted from its object, and used as a name for visions. Such ends are not happiness. But there is an end which men can seek and do find, which never deceives, which is real and tangible and felt to be happiness — and that end is pleasure. Pleasure is something we can be sure of, for it dwells not we know not where, but here in ourselves. It is found, and it can be found; it is the end for man and for beast, the one thing worth living for, the one thing they do live for and do really desire, and the only thing they ought to set before them. This is real, because we feel and know it to be real; and solely by partaking, or seeming to partake, in its reality do other ends pass for, and impose on the world as happiness."

We said that to answer the question, what happiness is, has been thought impossible; that there are few who, in the end, are unable to say what happiness is not. And if there be any one thing which well-nigh the whole voice of the world, from all ages, nations, and sorts of men, has agreed to declare is *not* happiness, that thing is pleasure and the search for it. Not in the school alone but round us in life, we see that to identify in the beginning pleasure and happiness leads in the end to the confession that there "is nothing in it," εὐδαιμονίαν ὅλως ἀδύνατον εἶναι.

The "pursuit of pleasure" is a phrase which calls for a smile or a sigh, since the world has learned that, if pleasure is the end, it is an end which must not be made one, and is found there most where it is not sought. If to find pleasure is the end and science is the means, then indeed we must say

> Die hohe Kraft
> Der Wissenschaft,
> Der ganzen Welt verborgen!
> Und wer nicht denkt,
> Dem wird sie geschenkt,
> Er hat sie ohne Sorgen.[1]

Common opinion repeats its old song that the search for pleasure is the coarsest form of vulgar delusion, that if you want to be happy in the sense of pleased you must not think of pleasure, but, taking up some accredited form of living, must make that your end, and in that case, with moderately good fortune, you will be happy; if you are not, then it must be your own fault; but that, if you go further, you are like to fare worse. You had better *not* try elsewhere, or, at least, not for pleasure elsewhere.

So far the weight of popular experience bears heavily against the practicability of Hedonism. But Hedonism, we shall be told, does not of necessity mean the search by the individual for the pleasure of the individual. It is to such selfish pleasure-seeking alone that the proverbial condemnation of Hedonism applies. The end for modern Utilitarianism is not the pleasure of one, but the pleasure of all, the maximum of pleasurable, and minimum of painful, feeling in all sentient organisms, and not in my sentient organism; and against the possibility of realizing such an end common opinion has nothing to say. This we admit to be true, but in this shape the question has never fairly come before the popular mind; and it would be well to remember that if the individual, when he seeks pleasure, fails in his individual aim, such a

---

[1] Thus rendered in Mr. C. Kegan Paul's version of *Faust*:

The highest might	But whosoe'er
Of science quite	Expends no care,
Is from the world concealed!	To him it is revealed.

fact ought at least to inspire us with some doubt whether, when mankind seek the pleasure of the sentient world, that end be so much more real and tangible.

Opinion, then, as the result of popular experience so far as it has touched on the question, would appear to be against the practicability of Hedonism. Still vulgar opinion must not count against philosophical theory, though it certainly may against the still more vulgar preconception as to the reality and palpable character of pleasure.

But Hedonism, we must remember, does not assert itself simply as a theory which can be worked. It puts itself forward as moral, as the one and only possible account of morality. The fact is the moral world, Hedonism is the supposed explanation; and if we find that non-theoretical persons, who have direct cognizance of the fact, with but few exceptions reject the explanation, that ought to have great weight with us. And the case stands thus undeniably. When moral persons without a theory on the matter are told that the moral end for the individual and the race is the getting a maximum surplusage of pleasurable feeling, and that there is nothing in the whole world which has the smallest moral value except this end and the means to it, there is no gainsaying that they repudiate such a result. They feel that there are things "we should choose even if no pleasure came from them"; and that if we choose these things, being good, for ourselves, then we must choose them also for the race, if we care for the race as we do for ourselves. We may be told, indeed, that a vulgar objection of this sort is founded on a misunderstanding, and to this we shall have to recur; but for the present we prefer to believe that never, except on a misunderstanding, has the moral consciousness in any case acquiesced in Hedonism. And we must say, I think, that supposing it possible that Hedonism could be worked, yet common moral opinion is decided against its being, what it professes to be, a sufficient account of morals.

For morality and religion believe in some end for the man and for the race to be worked out; some idea to be realized in mankind and in the individual, and to be realized even though it should not be compatible with the minimum of pain and maximum of pleasure in human souls and bodies, to say nothing at all about other sentient organisms. The end for our morality and our religion is an idea (or call it what you will), which is thought of both as the moving principle and final aim of human progress, and that idea (whatever else it may be, or may not be) most certainly is not the mere idea of an increase of pleasure and a diminution of pain. What we represent to ourselves as the goal of our being we must take as a law for the guidance alike both of this and that man, and of the race as a whole; and if you do not use the vague phrase "happiness," but say fairly and nakedly that you mean "feeling pleased as much as possible and as long as possible," then you cannot, I think, bring the Hedonistic end before the moral consciousness without a sharp collision.

Now I am not saying that what is commonly believed must be true. I am perfectly ready to consider the possibility of the ordinary moral creed being a mistaken one; but the point which I wish to emphasize is this: The fact is the moral world, both on its external side of the family, society, and the State, and the work of the individual in them, and again, on its internal side of moral feeling and belief. The theory which will account for and justify these facts as a whole is the true moral theory; and any theory which cannot account for these facts may in some other way, perhaps, be a very good and correct theory, but it is *not* a *moral* theory. Supposing every other ethical theory to be false, it does not follow that therefore Hedonism is a true ethical theory. It does not follow because it has refuted its "intuitive moralists" (or what not?) that therefore it accounts for the facts of the moral consciousness. Admitted that it is workable, it has still to be proved moral — moral in the sense of explaining, not explaining away morality. And it can be proved moral by the refuting of some other theory, only on the strength of two assumptions. The first is that there must be some existing theory which is a sufficient account of morals, and that is an unproved assumption; the second is that the disjunction, that the "either—or" of "intuitive" and "utilitarian" is complete and exhaustive, and that is a false assumption.[2]

[2] "Whoever would disprove the theory which makes utility our guide must produce another principle that were a surer and better guide.

At the cost of repetition, and perhaps of wearisomeness, I must dwell a little longer on the ordinary consciousness. There are times indeed when we feel that increase of progress means increase of pleasure and that it is hard to consider them apart. I do not mean those moments (if there are such) when the music-hall theory of life seems real to us, but the hours (and there must be such) when advance in goodness and knowledge, and in the pleasure of them, have been so intermingled together, and brought home as one to our minds (in our own case or in that of others), that we feel it impossible to choose one and not also choose the other. And there doubtless are hours again, when all that is called progress seems so futile and disappointing that we bitterly feel "increase of knowledge" is indeed "increase of sorrow," and that he who thinks least is happiest; when we envy the beasts their lives without a past or a future, their heedless joys and easily forgotten griefs; and when for ourselves, and if for ourselves then for others, we could wish to cease or be as they are *"von allem Wissensqualm entladen."* These are the extremes; but when in the season neither of our exaltation nor of our depression we soberly consider the matter, then we choose most certainly for ourselves (and so also for others) what we think the highest life, *i. e.*, the life with the highest functions; and in that life we certainly include the feeling of pleasure; but if the alternative is presented to us of lower functions with less pains and greater pleasures, or higher functions with greater pains and less pleasures, then we must choose the latter.

"Now if we reject *utility* as the index to God's commands, we must assent to the theory of hypothesis which supposes a *moral sense.* One of the adverse theories which regard the nature of that index is certainly true."— AUSTIN's *Jurisprudence*, I, 79.

If we wished to cross an unknown bog, and two men came to us, of whom the one said, "Some one must know the way over this bog, for there must be a way, and you see there is no one here beside us two, and therefore one of us two must be able to guide you. And the other man does not know the way, as you can soon see; therefore I must"—should we answer, "Lead on, I follow"? Philosophy would indeed be the easiest of studies if we might arrive at truth by assuming that one of two accounts must be true, and prove the one by disproving the other; but in philosophy this is just what cannot be done.

And the alternative is conceivable. If it is impossible in fact that a stage of progress could come where by advancing further in the direction of what seems to it highest, humanity would decrease its surplus of pleasure (and I do not see how it is to be proved impossible) [3] — yet, at all events, the alternative can be brought directly before the mind. Advance in this direction (the higher) at the cost of pleasure, on the whole, after the pleasure of advance is counted in; advance in that direction (the lower) with the gain of pleasure, on the whole, even after the regrets of the nonadvance have been subtracted. The necessity for choice can be imagined; and there is no doubt, on the one side, what the choice of the moral man would be; there is no doubt, on the other side, what, if pleasure were the end, it ought to be. In such a case, what we think the most moral man and people would be therefore the most certain to act immorally, if Hedonism is morality.

But these consequences, it will be urged, do not apply to modern Utilitarianism. That creed, we shall be told, whether for the man or the race is high and self-sacrificing. For not only does it place the end in the pleasure of all, not the pleasure of one; but in addition it distinguishes pleasures according to their quality. The greatest quantity of pleasure is not the end; there

[3] Mr. Mill's assertion that "most of the great positive evils of the world are in themselves removable" (*Utilitarianism*, p. 21), calls for no remark; but the reader may perhaps think that Mr. Spencer's doctrine of the Evanescence of Evil (*Social Statics*, p. 73, ff.) should be noticed. His proof seems (so far as I understand it) to rest on the following assumptions:

(1) The natural environment of mankind is stationary. Can this be proved?

(2) The spiritual environment of mankind is stationary. Not only can this not be proved, but the opposite is, or ought to be, supposed by the doctrine of evolution. Progress must alter the environment.

(3) Apparently children are to be born in harmony with their surroundings and remain so till death.

(4) Moral evil in the sense of moral badness, is to disappear. It will be impossible to oppose one's private good to the general good, and act according to the former. Self-will will cease and with it the pain it brings.

All these assumptions, I think, are wanted. Nos. 3 and 4 represent absolute impossibilities, so far as I understand the matter. No. 2 is impossible on the supposition of continual progress. No other supposition can be proved to be true; and No. 1 cannot, I believe, be proved. How far Mr. Spencer's own teaching contradicts these assumptions is of no importance here.

are pleasures we desire in preference to others even at the cost of discontent and dissatisfaction. These pleasures, then, are to be preferred, and these are the higher pleasures. Such a doctrine, it will be added, is surely moral.

The doctrine, we admit, has done homage to popular opinion, so far as, for the sake of it, to sacrifice its own consistency and desert its principle. This we shall have to prove later on. But yet we cannot for a moment think that it has succeeded in satisfying the demands of morality. Virtue is still a mere means to pleasure in ourselves or others and, as anything beyond, is worthless, if not immoral; is not virtue at all. What is right is determined by that which is most "grateful to the feelings" of connoisseurs in pleasures, who have tried them all. No compromise is possible on this point. Ordinary morality is clear that when it aims at virtue for itself and others, it has not got its eye on wages or perquisites; its motive, in the sense of the object of its conscious desire, is not the anticipated feeling of pleasure. What it has before its mind is an object, an act or an event, which is not (for itself at least) a state of the feeling self, in itself or others. To say that, in desiring the right, it proposes to itself a pleasure to be got by the right is to assert in the face of facts. To the moral mind that feeling is an accompaniment or a consequent and it may be thought of as such. But to think of it as more, to propose it as the end to which the act or objective event are the means, and nothing but the means, is simply to turn the moral point of view upside down. You may argue psychologically, if you will, and say that what is desired *is* pleasure (this is false, as we shall show in another Essay), and we are ready for argument's sake to admit it here; for here it makes not the smallest difference. The moral consciousness does not *think* it acts to get pleasure, and the point here at issue is not whether what it believes, and must believe, is or is not a psychological illusion, but whether Utilitarianism is in harmony therewith.

Hedonism in any form must teach "morality is a means to pleasure"; and whether that pleasure is to be got *in* morality or merely *by* morality, yet the getting of the pleasure is the ultimate aim. Pleasure for pleasure's sake is the end and nothing else is an end in any sense except so far as it is a means to pleasure. This, we repeat once more, is absolutely irreconcilable with ordinary moral beliefs. And not only is Hedonism repudiated by those beliefs as immoral, but as we saw, so far as the popular mind has pronounced upon it, it is also declared to be impracticable. These two points we wished to make clear, and with this result we have finished the first or introductory part of our undertaking.

It remains to ask in the second place, Why is it that pleasure-seeking as the search for my pleasure is declared vain, and pleasure itself impalpable and misleading, a something which gives us no standard to work by and no end to aim at, no system to realize in our lives? We must look for an answer to the nature of pleasure.

Pleasure and pain are feelings and they are nothing but feelings. It would perhaps be right to call them the two simple modes of *self*-feeling; but we are not here concerned with psychological accuracy. The point which we wish to emphasize and which we think is not doubtful is that, considered psychically, they are nothing whatever but states of the feeling self. This means that they exist in me only as long as I feel them, and only as I feel them, that beyond this they have no reference to anything else, no validity and no meaning whatever. They are "subjective" because they neither have, nor pretend to, reality beyond this or that subject. They are as they are felt to be, but they tell us nothing. In one word, they have no content; they are as states of us, but they have nothing for us.

I do not think it is necessary to dwell on this matter. Let us proceed to the application. The practical end, if it is to be a practical goal and standard, must present itself to us as some definite unity, some concrete whole that we can realize in our acts, and carry out in our life. And pleasure (as pain) we find to be nothing but a name which stands for a series of this, that, and the other feelings, which are not except in the moment or moments that they are felt, which have as a series neither limitation of number, beginning nor end, nor in themselves any reference at all, any of them, beyond themselves. To realize, as such, the self which feels pleasure and pain means to realize this infinite perishing series.[4] And it is clear at once that this is not what is required for a practical end. Let us see the problem a little closer.

On the one side our Hedonist is aware, however dimly, of himself not as this, nor that, nor the other particular feeling or satisfaction, but as something which is not this, that, or the other, and yet is real, and is to be realized. Self-realization, as we saw, was the object of desire; and so, as above, on the one hand is the self, which we are forced to look on as a whole which is in its parts, as a living totality, as a universal present throughout, and constituted by its particulars; and this self is setting out, however unaware, to find itself as such and to satisfy itself as such, or not to find itself and not to satisfy itself at all. On the other side is the mere feeling self, the series of particular satisfactions, which the self has come (how, we need not here inquire) to take as its reality and as the sole possible field for its self-realization.

The point to observe is the heterogeneous nature of the self to be satisfied, and of the proposed satisfaction, and the consequent impossibility of a solution for the problem. The practical difficulty is soon forced on the seeker after pleasure.

Pleasures, we saw, were a perishing series. This one comes and the intense self-feeling proclaims satisfaction. It is gone and *we* are not satisfied. It was not that one, then, but this one now; and this one now is gone. It was not that one, then, but another and another; but another and another do not give us what we want; we are still left eager and confident till the flush of feeling dies down, and when that is gone there is nothing left. We are where we began, so far as the getting happiness goes, and we have not found ourselves, and we are not satisfied.

This is common experience and it is the practical refutation of Hedonism or of the seeking happiness in pleasure. Happiness for the ordinary man neither means a pleasure nor a number of

---

[4] It is an abstraction, no doubt, to consider pleasurable feelings as mere pleasures, but it is not our abstraction but the Hedonist's. It is an abstraction, again, to consider feelings as merely particular. They cannot be that if they are *our* feelings, if they are the feelings of a self. But we can make our mere feeling self, as the self which feels mere pleasure and pain an object only in the series of its feelings, and these (as such a series) have no relations, each either within itself or beyond itself.

pleasures. It means in general the finding of himself or the satisfaction of himself as a whole, and in particular it means the realization of his concrete ideal of life. *"This* is happiness," he says, not identifying happiness with one pleasure or a number of them, but understanding by it, *"in* this is become fact what I have at heart." But the Hedonist has said, Happiness is pleasure, and the Hedonist knows that happiness is a whole.[5] How, then, if pleasures make no system, if they are a number of perishing particulars, can the whole that is sought be found in them? It is the old question, how find the universal in mere particulars? And the answer is the old answer, In their sum. The self is to be found, happiness is to be realized, in the sum of the moments of the feeling self. The practical direction is get *all* pleasures and you will have got happiness; and we saw above its well-known practical issue in weariness and dissatisfaction.

The theoretical reason is simple. The sum or the All of pleasures is a self-contradiction, and therefore the search for it is futile. A series which has no beginning, or, if a beginning yet no end, cannot be summed; there *is* no All, and yet the All is postulated, and the series is to be summed. But it cannot be summed till we are dead, and then, if we have realized it, we, I suppose, do not know it, and we are not happy; and before death we cannot have realized it, because there is always more to come, the series is always incomplete. What is the sum of pleasures and how many go to the sum? All of how many is it, and when

---

[5] I am quite aware that with *some* Hedonistic writers "happiness" is not distinguished from "pleasure." They are said to be simply the same. This is an outrage on language, which avenges itself in the confusion described below, footnote, p. 60. But the argument of the text is not affected by it. If happiness = pleasure, then "get happiness" = "get pleasure." What is pleasure? It is a general name, and "get happiness" will mean "get a general name." But a general name is not a reality, and cannot be got. The reality is the particular. "Get happiness" will mean then, "get some one pleasure." Is that it? No, we are to get all the happiness we can. And so, after all our quibbling, "get happiness" *does* mean "get the largest possible sum or collection of pleasures." Mr. Green, in his Introduction to Hume's *Treatise* (II, 7), has made this so clear that one might have hoped it could not have been misunderstood. On the whole subject of this Essay let me recommend the student to consult him.

are we at the end? After death or in life? Do you mean a finite number? Then more is beyond. Do you mean an infinite number? Then we never reach it; for a further pleasure is conceivable, and nothing is infinite which has something still left outside of it. We must say, then, that no one ever reaches happiness. Or do you mean as much pleasure as a man can get? Then every one at every point is happy and happiness is always complete, for, by the Hedonistic theory, we all of us get as much as we can.[6]

[6] I am anxious that the reader should not pass by this argument as a verbal puzzle. Beside it there is certainly much more to be said against Hedonism; but the root of Hedonism is not understood, until it is seen (1) that pleasure, as such, is an abstraction (cf. Essay VII); (2) that the sum of pleasures is a fiction. On this latter head I fear that I must further enlarge.

"Get all you can" is a familiar phrase, and is very good sense. I say to a boy, "Go into that room and fetch out all the apples you can carry"; and there is no nonsense in that. There is a given finite sum of apples, which I do not know, but which, under all the conditions, is the maximum. This is got and brought, and the task is accomplished. Why then not say, "Get all the pleasures you can"? For these reasons. (a) Let it be granted that there is a given finite sum of pleasures for the man to get; yet *he* never *has* it. Only death puts an end to the work; and after death nothing, or the same unfinished task. (b) There is really no such sum. A pleasure *is* only in the time during which I feel it. A past pleasure means either an idea, or *another* (secondary) impression. *Itself* is nothing at all; I did get it, I have not got it; and the "did get" is not the pleasure. In order to have the sum of pleasures, I must have them all *now*, which is impossible. Thus you cannot reach the end, and the effort to reach it is not in itself desirable. You may say, if you please, The end is an illusion, and the effort worthless in itself, but this particular effort gives a specific pleasure, which is the end. But if you do this, then you either (i) sink considerations of quantity, and the *greatest* happiness principle is given up; or (ii) the same problem as above breaks out with respect to the sum of specific pleasures.

If you admit that to get the greatest sum in life is unmeaning, then arises the question, Can you approximate, and make approximation the end? I will not raise the question, Can you approximate to a confessed fiction? and to avoid that, let us say, The end is for me, at any given moment of life, to be having then the greatest possible number of units of pleasure. Here we fall into the dilemma given in the text. Either happiness is never reached, or there is no one who does not reach the most perfect happiness imaginable.

(1) *If* happiness means the greatest possible number of units then I *never* reach it. Whatever I have is finite, and beyond every finite sum another unit is conceivable.

The Hedonist has taken the universal in the sense of all the particulars, and in this sense, here as everywhere, since the particulars are arising and perishing, the universal has no truth nor reality. The true universal, which unconsciously he seeks, is infinite, for it is a concrete whole concluded within itself, and complete; but the false universal is infinite in the sense of a process *ad indefinitum*. It is a demand for, a would-be, completeness, with everlasting present incompleteness. It is always finite, and so never is realized. The sum is never finished; when the last pleasure is reached we stand no nearer our end than at the first. It would be so, even if the pleasures did not die; but in addition the past pleasures have died; and we stand with heart unsatisfied and hands empty, driven on and beyond forever in pursuit of a delusion, through a weary round which never advances. There remains, then, to Hedonism either the assertion that happiness is completed in one intense moment, or the confession that happiness is impossible, or the attempt to place it elsewhere than in the sum of pleasures.

The first is the *"nullo vivere consilio."* It is the giving up of

(2) *If* happiness means having all I can get, no matter how much or how little, then, given the truth of the common Hedonistic psychology, every man at every moment has absolute happiness. This is very obvious. "Why so?" comes the objection, "if Mr. A. had done otherwise he would have had more pleasure." "You mean," I answer, "*If* he had been Mr. B." When, in ordinary language, we say, "He did not do what he could, or what was possible," we mean, "His energy did expend itself in this direction, failed to do so in that," and we impute inability as a fault, where it is the result of previous misdirection. But the common Hedonist cannot say this, because, according to him, there is only one possible direction of expenditure, *i. e.*, the greatest seeming pleasure. You have no choice between pleasure and something else, you can do nothing but gravitate to what seems most pleasant, and you cannot alter what seems except by your will, *i. e.*, by gravitation to what seems most pleasant. Every one has done his conceivable utmost to approximate and therefore is absolutely happy.

I think the better plan for the Hedonist would be to make happiness a fixed finite sum, which can be got, and beyond which nothing counts; and similarly to fix an unhappiness point on the scale; but we have pursued the subject far enough.

The question of the approximative character of all morality will be discussed in another place.

any practical goal or any rule of life, and we are not called upon to consider it further. The second is inevitable if happiness is equal to the sum, or the greatest possible amount, of pleasures; for one and the other are the same unreal fiction. The end, in this sense, exists only in the head of the Hedonistic moral man. His morality is the striving to realize an idea which can never be realized, and which, if realized, would be *ipso facto* annihilated. He would feel it no objection to his theory nor any comfort in his sorrow if we said to him that, if happiness could be, then the tale would be made up, the end would be reached, the search would be over, and with it all morality; for his morality is nothing to him as an end but only as a means; and the bitterness of his lot is filled up by the thought that the means he does not care for are always with him, and the end he lusts after away from him. His morality says, get what you never can get; never rest, never be satisfied, strive beyond the present to an impossible future.

The above is the proverbial experience of the voluptuary. His road to happiness is well known to be the worst, since pleasure there cannot be where there is no satisfaction; and he must end (whatever else may become of him) by giving up his earnest search for the sum of pleasures.

The third alternative is not to give up pleasure as an end, but to place happiness elsewhere than in the greatest possible amount of "grateful feeling." This is what the prudent man of the world, with a love for pleasure, generally does do. We take a certain quantity of pleasure, and absence of pain, as a fair amount, which we may call happiness, because we feel we can do with it; and to get this amount we take up some way of living, which we follow, in general without thinking of pleasure. If opportunity offers for delights by the way, we take them, but without inconveniencing ourselves, without leaving the road too far, and without thinking too much about it. It is a good rule to get more, but a rule we must not make too much of, or follow to the point of endangering our happiness, *i. e.*, the fixed and fair amount which comes to us from our course of life.

Pleasure is still ostensibly the end; but really it has ceased to be so, and, whether we know it or not, our way of living is an end to our minds and not a mere means. In short, we have got interests and these are objects of desire not thought of as means to pleasure. We have adopted happiness in the vulgar sense and really have given up Hedonism as the consistent hunt after pleasure for pleasure's sake. Yet pleasure is still nominally the end, and hence the above view of life lies open to the following objections:

"You tell me that pleasure is my end; and yet you tell me not to make it my end but to make some accredited type of life my end, and take the pleasure as it comes from that. I am to make getting pleasure my aim, though only by the way and at odd times. And in this manner you assure me that, in the long run, I shall secure the greatest amount of pleasurable feeling. It seems strange to have a mark one must not look at, but I should not care for that if I were sure to hit. Yet this is what I cannot tell if I shall do. I see men die, having reaped for themselves a harvest of painful self-denial; and the pleasure they made by it was but gleanings for others, when they were in the grave. Did they attain their end? And I, since our life at any moment may cheat us, shall I put off a present certainty for the sake of a doubtful future?"

The answer must be, That is true enough; there is no certainty in life, but still it is more reasonable to act on probabilities. You may die, but the chances are you will live. You had better suppose that it will be so, and, taking the rules for living, the moral "Nautical Almanack,"[7] direct your course by them; for, if you live as long as most men, you will certainly in this way get the most pleasure.

And perhaps this answer may satisfy. But a new and serious difficulty arises. It being admitted that life is to be regulated on probabilities, the question then occurs, Who is to judge for the probabilities? The moral end is for me to get the most pleasure I can; the moral rule is, "Act on the probability of your living, and therefore live for life as a whole"; but this moral rule tells me nothing about the moral Almanack. Why is that to be to me a law? What does it rest upon? What others have done and found? Will others be responsible for me, then? Am I to act upon my own opinion, or am I to follow the Almanack even

[7] J. S. Mill, *Utilitarianism*, p. 36.

against my opinion? Is the latter course right and justifiable? Will it, so to speak, excuse me in the Hedonistic judgment-day when charged with having missed my end by misconduct, to plead that I did what others did, and that, when my own belief would have brought me right, I followed the multitude, and therefore did evil?

It appears to me that, if I am to seek my pleasure, it must be left to me to judge concerning my pleasure; and, this being so, the Almanack is not a law to me. It was made to be used by me according to my private views, not to be followed against them. And herewith all moral legislation disappears.

For obviously, (1) circumstances get into strange tangles which cannot be provided against; and the course laid down in the Almanack as a law may, in peculiar cases, lead to pain instead of pleasure; and here I must disregard the Almanack. And obviously, (2) not outward situations only, but men's temperaments differ. What brings pleasure to one brings none to another; and so with pain. You can speak generally beforehand, but it may not apply to this or that man. And the consequence is that the Almanack and its moral rules are no authority. It is right to act according to them. It is right to act diametrically against them. In short, they are not laws at all; they are only rules, and rules, as we know, admit of and imply exceptions. As Mr. Stephen has said: "A given road may be the direct way from one place to another, but that fact is no reason for following the road when you are offered a short cut. It may be a good rule not to seek for more than 5 per cent in investments, but if it so happens that you can invest at 10 per cent with perfect safety, would not a man who refused to do so be a fool?"[8]

And with this, if Hedonism be taken as the seeking my private pleasure, we have come to the end of Hedonism as a practical creed. Its aim was the getting for myself a maximum surplus of pleasurable feeling, and it gave me rules which it was my duty to

[8] F. Stephen, *Liberty, Equality, and Fraternity,* 2nd ed., p. 363. Mr. Stephen has put this part of the case so strongly that I have not thought it worth while to enlarge upon it. Kant is very clear and successful on this point.

follow. But it is not in earnest with its rules; they may hold good or they may not hold good; I may keep them or break them, whichever I think most likely to issue in pleasure in my particular case. And it is not in earnest with its end. To aim at pleasure is not to get it, and yet the getting of it is a moral duty. We must aim at it then by the way, without caring or trying too much to get it. We are not to think about the rules except as servants which may be useful or worthless, and about the end, perhaps, the less we think the better. We are to please ourselves about the rules; we are to please ourselves about the end; for end and rules are neither end nor rules. Our positive aim in life is given up; we may content ourselves, as a substitute, with the resolve to live our life as we find it, to sink useless theories, and follow the bent of our practical leanings; or, saddened at our disenchantment, may embrace the conclusion that, if pleasure cannot be found, yet pain at least can be avoided. Not only in the school, but in life around us, does the positive beginning conduct to the negative result, to the making a goal of an absence, to the placing the end in a mere negation.

We have shown, in the first place, the collision between popular opinion and Hedonism as the search for pleasure; we have shown, in the second place, the reason why the seeking of *my* pleasure gives no practical end in life. On both points we have dwelt, perhaps, at unnecessary length; but we have not yet done justice to the doctrine which makes virtue a means, not to my pleasure, but to the pleasure of the "whole sentient creation"—to modern Utilitarianism which may be called, I suppose, our most fashionable moral philosophy. This we must now notice, but only so far as our subject compels us. A more detailed examination is not called for here, and, as we think, would not repay us anywhere.

The end, as before, is the greatest amount of pleasurable feeling, yet not now in me, but in the sentient world as a whole. The first thing to observe is that (as we noticed above), if happiness means this, happiness is unrealizable—it can by no possibility be reached. If the greatest happiness, in the sense of the maximum of pleasure, was, as applied to the individual, a mere "idea" or rather a self-contradictory attempt at an idea, which we saw by its very nature could not exist as a fact, then *a fortiori*, I should say, the realization of a maximum of pleasure in the "whole sentient creation" (which stands, I suppose, for what particular animal organisms are now and are to be hereafter), is nothing but a wild and impossible fiction.

Happiness, in the sense of "as much as you can," we saw, is never and nowhere realized; or, if anyone prefers it, is realized everywhere and without any drawback. In both cases, as a something set to be gained, it has no signification. Happiness in the meaning of a maximum of pleasure can never be reached; and what is the sense of trying to reach the impossible? Happiness, in the meaning of always a little more and always a little less, is the stone of Sisyphus and the vessel of the Danaides—it is not heaven, but hell. Whether we try for it or not, we always have got a little more and a little less[9] (than we might have), and never at any time, however much we try for it, can we have a little more or a little less than we have got.

But theoretical considerations of this sort are likely neither to be understood nor regarded. Our morality, we shall hear, "is a practical matter." And I should have thought it indeed a practical consideration, whether our chief good be realizable or no, whether it be πρακτὸν καὶ κτητὸν ἀνθρώπῳ or exist only in the heads of certain theorists. But let this pass. We can avoid, I dare say, practical inconvenience by not meaning what we say or saying what we mean.

Whatever, then, we may think about the possibility of the actual existence of the end, and the satisfactoriness (or otherwise) of aiming at the impossible and unmeaning, at all events our moral law and precept is clear. Increase the pleasure, *i. e.*, multiply in number, and intensify in quality, the pleasurable feelings of sentient beings, and do the opposite by their pains.

We have already noticed, but it may not be amiss to call

[9] To define happiness as "increase in pleasure," or "the having more than we had," would not extricate us from our difficulties. For then no stationary state could be happy at all, and no man would be happier than another save in respect of being in more intense transition. The actual amount of pleasure would go for nothing. But it is not worth while to develop the absurdities consequent on such a possible definition.

attention once more to the fact that a doctrine of this sort is directly opposed to popular morality. If, by being changed into pigs, we secured an absolute certainty of a greater amount of pleasure with a less amount of pain, we (I speak for the ordinary person) should decline the change, either for ourselves or the race, and should think it our duty to do so. But, if we believe that the greatest amount of pleasure is the end, it would be our duty to strive after and accept such a change. And some such choice is not a mere theoretical possibility. Unless Fourier be much belied, his scheme of "phalansteries" was a practical proposal to seek for pleasure as the end, and all else as means. The ordinary moral man refuses to discuss such a proposal. He repudiates the end, and the means with it. But the "greatest amount of pleasure" doctrine must accept the end and calmly discuss the means; and this is not the moral point of view. It is surely imaginable (I do not say it is likely), that we might have to say to a large and immoral majority, "If I wanted to make you happy, which I do not, I should do so by pampering your vices, which I will not."[10]

So much for the morality of the theory. Let us now consider its practicability and consistency. The end, as the pleasure of all, is, like my pleasure, not something which I can apprehend and carry out in my life. It is not a system, not a concrete whole. There are no means included in it; there are none which, in themselves, belong to the end. Wanting to know what I am to do, "Increase the pleasure of all" gives me, by itself, no answer. "But there is no need that it should," will be the reply. The experience of mankind has discovered the means which tend to increase pleasure; these are laid down in the moral Almanack (Mill, p. 36), and they may fairly be considered as included in the end.

Here I think that Hedonism does not see a most serious difficulty. It is the old question, What is the nature of the authority of the Almanack, and are its rules laws? If they are laws, on what do they rest? If they are not, are there any other moral laws; and without laws can you have morality? Let me explain the objection. You cannot, I object to the Hedonist, make these laws part of the end, and identify them therewith; for the

[10] F. Stephen, *Liberty, Equality, and Fraternity*, p. 287.

end was clearly laid down as pleasurable feeling and there is no essential connection between that end and the laws as means. If the laws or rules are not feelings (and they are not), they must be mere means to feeling. The relation of the two, of the end and the means, is external. You cannot, from the conception of the end as such, conclude in any way to the rules as such. This seems to me quite clear; and, if it is so, then you can in your mind put the end on one side and the rules on the other, and contemplate the possibility of going to the end without these particular means. You may say you do not care for possibilities; experience shows the connection of means and end, and that is enough. This point I wish especially to emphasize: such an observed connection is not sufficient; or it is sufficient only if we are prepared to make one of the two following assumptions. The first is that the general opinion of mankind, which we suppose to exist and be embodied in these rules, is infallible; that it takes the only way, or the best way, to the given end; and also that I have no excuse for thinking otherwise. The second is that, whether I think the rules the best means to the end or not, I have in any case to sink my own view as to the right means to the given end, and take the rules as something which is not to be departed from. One of these two supposable assumptions is necessary.

(1) Now with respect to the first, I see no ground upon which the Hedonist, were he so disposed, could maintain and justify such a strong asssertion of the ὃ πᾶσι δοκεῖ. Why am I bound to consider these laws infallible, in such a sense that any departure from them, in any case, must contribute less to the given end than a corresponding observance? And how to me is such a truth (if it be a truth) not to be an open question? How is my doubt or my denial of the truth to be *ipso facto* immorality? An example will help us. Let us take the precept, Do not commit adultery. How are we to prove that no possible adultery can increase the overplus of pleasurable feeling? How are we to show that a man's honest and probable view to the contrary is an immoral view? And, if we cannot show these things, what becomes of this first supposable assumption?

(2) Then, if mankind may err, if the right of private judgment

is not to be suppressed, if the supposed general experience is not infallible, how can it be moral for me always to follow it even in the teeth of my own judgment? I may be perfectly aware that acting on rules is, speaking generally, the way to reach the end. I may even admit that the departure from rules in most cases has produced, and must produce, an effect detrimental to the end. I might, if I pleased, for argument's sake admit (though it would be contrary to fact, and no one could ask for such an admission) that every previous departure from rules has been a failure, and has decreased the surplus. But now the matter stands thus: I have taken all pains to form an opinion, and I am quite certain that my case is an exception. I have no doubt whatever that in this instance the breaking of a rule will increase the surplus. To say that I am a fool does not touch the question; to say that I must be mistaken does not touch the question; to say that I ought not to think as I do, or ought not to act accordingly, begs the question. The moral end is clear; I, after having thought over all considerations up to my lights, am clear as to the means. What right have you, what right has the world to tell me to hold my hand, to make your uncertain opinion the standard rather than the certain end? How shall I answer for it to my own conscience[11] if I do? What is this rule that is to come between me and my moral duty? Let us repeat our illustration. The rule says, Do not commit adultery. I wish to commit adultery. I am sure I do not want to please myself at all, in fact rather the contrary. I am as positive as I can be of anything, that the case is either not contemplated by the rule, or, if it is, that the rule is wrong, that the proposed act must diminish the sum of the pain, and must increase the sum of the pleasure of the sentient world as a whole, and this too after all consequences that I can reckon (and I can reckon no more) have been counted in. Is it immoral then to break the rule; or rather is it not immoral to keep it, to sacrifice a real good to a mere idea? My conscience is clear; and my dreams will not be broken by "the groans of an abstraction."[12]

[11] "And to my God," I might add, against those who drag the Deity into the question.

[12] J. S. Mill, *Dissertations and Discussions*, I, 21.

Now, if it be answered here that, on any theory of morals, collisions must arise—that I fully admit to be true: and again, that on any theory collisions *of this kind* must arise (*i.e.*, not the conflict of moral ends, but the conflict of diverse reflective calculations as to the means to a given moral end)—that (though I absolutely deny it) I will admit for argument's sake, and argument's sake alone. But (1) it belongs to the essence of Hedonism to provoke such collisions, and to justify the raising of casuistical questions on well-nigh every point of conduct, and this not merely theoretically, but with a view to one's own immediate practice. The reason is simple, and we have stated it already. The end for Hedonism has no means which belong to it and are inseparable from it. The means are external and so long as you get the end the means are immaterial. The relation of the means to the end is matter of opinion, and it cannot be more than matter of opinion. The opinion of any number of persons is still only an opinion. The end I am certain of. As to the means, I have nothing but the opinion of myself and others. The last appeal is to my private judgment. Now my private judgment may assure me that in 999 cases out of 1000 it contributes more to the end that I should not exercise my private judgment. It *may* assure me that, being what I am, it will contribute to the surplus if I never use my private judgment. But it need not so assure me. It may assure me that in the thousandth case I had better use my private judgment. And it may go a great deal further than this. The question is not, *Do* I and others act as a rule from habit, and according to general opinion? for that is a mere question of fact. The question is one of morals: *ought* my private judgment ever to come into collision with general opinion, as in fact it sometimes does and must? If not, why not? If it may, then ought I in such cases ever to follow it? and, if not, why not? If I may follow it in my own case once, why not twice? If here, why not there? And if anybody is ever to use their private judgment on any moral point, why may not I be the man, and this the case where I may? To put the whole matter in two words—the precepts of Hedonism are only rules, and rules may always have exceptions. They are not, and, so far as I see, they cannot be made to be laws. I am not their servant but they are mine. And, so far as my lights go, this is to make possible, to justify, and even to encourage, an incessant practical casuistry; and that, it need scarcely be added, is the death of morality. Before I proceed, however, let me entreat the reader to remember that the question, Are Utilitarians immoral? is one question, and the question, Is their theory immoral? altogether another and the only one which we are concerned with.

And (2), if it were true that no other moral theory was in a happier plight, what are we to say but "so much the worse for all moral theories," and not "so much the better for Hedonism." The moral consciousness is the touchstone of moral theories, and that moral consciousness, I appeal to it in every man, has laws which are a great deal more than rules. To that consciousness "Do not commit adultery" is a law to be obeyed; it is not the prescription of a more or less questionable policy. It is not a means, which in the opinion of A, B, and C will or may conduce to an end other than itself, and in the opinion of D may or will not do so. Let the Hedonist refute thrice or four times over, if he pleases, his rival theories; but he does not thereby establish his own, and is no nearer doing so than before.

To proceed—the conclusion we have reached is that, supposing it to be certain that the end is the maximum surplus of pleasure in the sentient world, that end gives no standard for morality. The end is in itself most abstract and impalpable. The means are external and in themselves immaterial to the end; and the fixing the relation of means to end must always be matter of opinion; in the last resort it is, and (what is most important) it *ought* to be, matter of my private opinion. As it turned out before, so here also the rules are not laws; I can please myself about them; and a standard which is no standard, a law which is no law, but which I may break or keep, which is at the mercy of changing judgment and fleeting opinion, is no practical basis for me to regulate my life by.[13]

[13] To bring the matter home to the reader, I will produce an example or two of cases where Hedonism gives no guidance. If in certain South Sea Islands the people have not what we call "morality," but are very happy, is

The Utilitarian, I am perfectly aware, does not wish me to keep the end continually before me, but rather to have my eye on the accredited means. The question is not, however, what the Utilitarian wishes, but what his theory justifies and demands. One of the most serious objections to Hedonism is that, as we have seen, it is not in earnest with its own conclusions. It is no argument in favor of a theory, it is surely rather an argument against it, that it cannot teach the legitimate consequences of its principles.

The greatest amount of pleasure then, if we take it for our end, we have found to be unrealizable, to be non- or im-moral, and

it moral or immoral to attempt to turn them from their ways? If by an immoral act, which probably will not be discovered, I can defeat a stroke of pernicious policy on a large scale, what am I to do? Is prostitution a good or a bad thing? To prove that it is bad we must prove that it diminishes the surplus of pleasant sensations, and is not this a fair subject for argument? Do I or do I not add to the surplus of "grateful feeling" by a given act or acts of sexual irregularity? This is a serious practical question, and I know that in many cases it is honestly answered in the affirmative; and in some of these cases, so far as such impalpable questions can be judged of, I should say the affirmation was correct. Is suicide ever allowable, and if so, when? and when not? Is murder, and if not, why not? and so on with all the crimes in the decalog and out of it. If any given act is to be shown immoral you must, if called on, exhibit the probability of its producing more pain than pleasure in the world, and is not this again and again a hopeless problem? Of course the Hedonist does not *want* the question raised. Of course he *wants* people to go by rules always, and that no one should ask any questions, except it be himself. That we quite understand. The point is, if I *choose* to raise such questions, on what ground can he say I may not? On what ground can he refuse to discuss the case? On what ground can he blame me if I take and act on a view which is other than his view?

"The beliefs which have thus come down are the rules of morality for the multitude, and for the philosopher until he has succeeded in finding better. That philosophers might easily do this, even now, on many subjects . . . . I admit, or rather earnestly maintain" (Mill, *Util.*, p. 34). From the author of the *Essay on Liberty* this should mean a good deal. If the philosopher may make new rules, I suppose he may modify old ones. And who is "the philosopher"? Are we (as proposed for the franchise) to have an examination, passing in which shall entitle a man to try "experiments in living"? Or shall we leave it to private judgment? Then I should like to know in these days of "advanced thinking" who would *not* be a "philosopher," and how many would be left in the "multitude."

lastly in practice to be an unworkable doctrine. All this time
we have taken the end for granted. But now we are to ask, What
ground is there for taking the pleasure of the sentient creation as
the moral end? What possible reason is there why I should look
on this as that for which everything else must be given up, even
my own pleasure and my own life? And here I think Hedonism
is altogether helpless. The consistent, and the only consistent
position, is to say that I desire my own pleasure, that the pleasure
of others is in many ways conducive to my own, and that desiring
the end I must desire the means also. But this is a return to the
doctrine we discussed above, viz., that my pleasure is the end;
and to accept this doctrine is to leave the standpoint of modern
Utilitarianism, and to say, Its end is not an end; it is or it may
be a mere means.

The Hedonist in his distress may turn himself in various
directions.

(1) He may say, "The end is not provable because too good to
be provable. It is self-evident, and nothing else is more certain."
But having noticed already that the moral consciousness repudiates the claim of his end to be the chief good, and it being clear
that selfishness often in its practice, and sometimes in its theory,
rejects its claim to be anything more than a means, I think we need
not trouble ourselves with its pretense to self-evidence; more
especially as, according to the psychology of the ordinary Hedonist, to desire the end as such is a psychological impossibility.

(2) The next resource is the *Deus ex machina*. Not only on a
certain stage, but also with certain theorists the maxim seems to
hold good, "When in trouble bring in the Deity." God, we shall be
told, wills the greatest amount of pleasure of the whole sentient
creation, and therefore we ought to do so likewise. Now, even if I
were capable of it, I am not disposed to enter into the speculative
theology of our "inductive" moralists; I will say to them merely,
Lasst unsern Herrgott aus dem Spass, and go on.

(3) But now I have to meet no less an antagonist than Mr.
Mill himself; and he has proved that the Utilitarian end is
desirable. Let us hear him:

"No reason can be given why the general happiness is desirable except that each person, so far as he believes it to be attainable, desires his own happiness. This, however, being a fact, we have not only all the proof which the case admits of, but all which it is possible to require, that happiness is a good; that each person's happiness is a good to that person, and the general happiness, therefore, a good to the aggregate of all persons" (*Util.*, p. 52)

Whether our "great modern logician" thought that by this he had proved that the happiness of all was desirable for each, I will not undertake to say. He either meant to prove this, or has proved what he started with, viz., that each desires his own pleasure. And yet there is a certain plausibility about it. If many pigs are fed at one trough, each desires his own food, and somehow as a consequence does seem to desire the food of all; and by parity of reasoning it should follow that each pig, desiring his own pleasure, desires also the pleasure of all. But as this scarcely seems conformable to experience, I suppose there must be something wrong with the argument, and so likewise with the argument of our philosopher.[14]

The End as the pleasure of all is, starting from the theories of our Utilitarian moralists, not only unprovable but impossible. If my self is something which exists by itself and independent of other selves, if all that I desire and can desire is my pleasure, and if that pleasure is an isolated feeling of this particular self, then the sole desirable is a state or states of my own feeling, and in the second place whatever is a means to that. To desire an object which is not the idea of my pleasure is psychologically impossible, and no torturing and twisting of phrases will make a connection from such an idea to any such object. And such an object is the idea of the pleasure of others considered not as conducing to mine. I may happen to desire the pleasure of others, and I may happen not to do so. To tell me the pleasure of others is desirable for me is to tell me you think it will conduce to my own; to tell

[14] Either Mill meant to argue, "*Because* everybody desires his own pleasure, *therefore* everybody desires his own pleasure"; or, "*Because* everybody desires his own pleasure, *therefore* everybody desires the pleasure of everybody else." Disciples may take their choice. To us it matters not which interpretation be correct. In the one case Mill has proved his point by a pitiable sophism; in the other he has not proved any point at all.

me I ought to desire it either says that again, or it is nonsense. Ought is the feeling of obligation, and "when the feeling ceases the obligation ceases." The Utilitarian believes on psychological grounds that pleasure is the sole desirable; he believes on the strength of his natural and moral instincts that he must live for others; he puts the two together, and concludes that the pleasure of others is what he has to live for. This is not a good theoretical deduction,[15] but it is the generation of the Utilitarian monster, and of that we must say that its heart is in the right place but the brain is wanting.

Its heart, its "natural sentiment," does tell it that its substance is one with the substance of its fellows; that in itself and by itself it is not itself at all, and has no validity except as a violent and futile attempt at abstraction. And yet if we deny that a universal can be more than "an idea," if we are sure that the merely individual and the real are one and the same, and in particular that the self is exclusive of other selves, and is in this sense a mere individual; and if further, for morality at all events, we cannot

[15] It is monstrous to argue thus: "Because (1) on psychological grounds it is certain that we can desire nothing but our own private pleasure; because (2) on some other grounds something *else* (whatever it may be), something not my feeling of pleasure, something other than my private self, is desired and desirable; therefore (3) this something else which is desired and desirable is the pleasure of others, since by (1), only pleasure can be desired." If we argue in this way, we may well go a little further to "(4) and therefore we can and do desire something not our own private pleasure, and therefore (1) is false, and therefore the whole argument disappears since it is upon (1) that the whole rests."

I am ashamed to have to examine such reasoning but it is necessary to do so since it is common enough. Is it not palpable at first sight that (1) and (2) are absolutely incompatible, that each contradicts the other flatly? You must choose between them, and, whichever you choose, the proof of Utilitarianism goes, because that springs from the unnatural conjunction of both.

The only escape that I can see is to say in (2) that something is desirable though not desired, and write "not desired but desirable" for "desired and desirable." But not only is this perhaps altogether unmeaning, but also the conclusion now disappears; you can get nothing from the premises. Because A is desired and B is desirable, it does not follow, I suppose, that a hash of A and B is desired and desirable.

do without something that is universal, something which is wider
and stronger than this or that self—then here, as in all other
spheres, we are face to face with the problem, How out of mere
individuals (particulars), which are fixed as such, can you get a
universal? And the problem put in this way is insoluble. The
self can desire in the end, as we too think, nothing but itself,
and if the self it is to realize is an atom, a unit which repels
other units, and can have nothing in itself but what is exclusively
its, its feeling, its pleasure and pain—then it is certain that it can
stand to others, with their pleasures and pains, only in an external
relation; and since it is the end, the others must be the means,
and nothing but the means. On such a basis morality is impossible; and yet morality does exist. But if the head could follow
the heart, not with a wretched compromise but altogether; if the
self to be realized is not exclusive of other selves, but on the
contrary is determined, characterized, made what it is by relation
to others; if my self which I aim at is the realization in me of a
moral world which is a system of selves, an organism in which
I am a member, and in whose life I live—then I cannot aim at
my own well-being without aiming at that of others. The others
are not mere means to me, but are involved in my essence; and
this essence of myself, which is not only mine but embraces and
stands above both me and this man and the other man, is superior
to and gives a law to us all, in a higher sense than the organism
as a whole gives a law to the members. And this concrete and real
universal makes the morality, which does exist, possible in theory
as well as real in fact. It is this which modern Utilitarianism
is blindly groping after, but it will not find it till it gives
up the Hedonism of its end and the basis of its psychology which
stands upon uncriticized, violent, and unreal metaphysical abstractions.

So much in passing, and here we might well end. We have
dwelt too long on the efforts of Hedonism to compromise with
morality, but we are forced to notice one last attempt. This consists in distinguishing pleasures, according to their quality,[16] into

[16] There is a point which might be raised here, and which is of considerable
importance. It is this. Are pleasures, *as* pleasures, distinguishable by anything else than quantity? The pleasure, as such, is not the whole pleasant

higher and lower. The former are superior, the latter are inferior; and hence, in preferring the higher pleasures, we are true to Hedonism and yet are at one with the moral consciousness. We must briefly examine this doctrine.

It has two forms. One of these takes quality simply as quality; the other takes quality in relation to quantity, and looks on it as the index or result of quantity. The latter, we shall find, keeps true to the principle of the greatest surplus of pleasure, but it says nothing new. The former leaves the principle unawares and moves unknowingly to other ground, but can get no standing-place for morality. Let us first discuss the latter; but, before we begin, we must call attention to the phrases "higher" and "lower."

Higher and lower (forgive me, dear reader) are "relative"— they are comparatives and they hence mean more or less of something. Higher means nearer some top, or it means nothing. Lower means nearer some bottom, or it means nothing. This being established, when we talk of "higher" and "lower" pleasure, we ought to know what our top and our bottom are, or else we risk talking nonsense.

Next let me observe (and forgive me, if you can, reader) that top and bottom, as a rule, are "relative," and depend on the way in which you look at the matter. If the top is the "end," you may put the end anywhere—benevolence is (morally) higher than

feeling, not the whole of *what* is felt. Then we have to ask, Does this *"what* is felt,"* which qualifies the pleasure, and makes it of one sort and not of another, make part of the mere pleasure itself, *as* pleasure? Or have we to say, Pleasure is itself always one and the same, and differs only in degree; sorts of pleasures are degrees of the same pleasure in reference to sorts of other feelings, which, as such, are *not* pleasures as such? Or more briefly, Has pleasure any content in itself? If not, then it has no qualitative distinctness in itself, but only by its reference to that which it goes with. Is not pleasure, as such, the abstraction of one element of a whole psychical state from that state; and when so abstracted, are there differences of *kind* in it, or only of degree? Not wishing to give a positive opinion on this point, I have not introduced it into the text as affecting the argument. But the thoughtful reader will at once perceive its bearing. Hedonism, when it ceases to aim at pleasure as such and nothing but pleasure, is false to its principle and becomes incoherent. But if pleasure, as such, is not qualitatively distinguishable, then we must have regard to nothing but quantity.

selfishness, murder is higher (as a crime) than larceny. You may speak of the height of goodness, badness, pleasure, pain, beauty, and ugliness. And so, when a man talks to us of "higher" and "lower," he says nothing to us at all till we know what end or summit he has in his mind.

Again, higher and lower, as comparative terms, refer to degree. What is higher has a greater degree (or it has a greater number of degrees) of something definite; what is lower has a less degree or number of degrees. Their quality, as higher and lower, is referable to quantity.[17] So that apart from quantity, apart from degree, there is no comparison, no estimation, no higher and lower at all.

The result of these perhaps trivial considerations is that if we are confined to *mere* quality, the words higher and lower have no meaning. If of two pleasures I cannot say one is higher than the other in degree (as intenser), or as the result or producer of degree (as accompaniment of higher function, or as connected with approximation to some end), then the words higher and lower cannot be applied to them. The sphere of mere quality is the world of immediate perception; and here we may say A or we may say B, but we cannot make comparisons between A and B without leaving our sphere. I may take this and not that, I may choose that and not the other, but if, because of this and on the mere strength of this I call one higher and one lower, I am not simply arbitrary and perhaps wrong in my opinion, but I am talking sheer and absolute nonsense.

To proceed then with one of our two views, (1) the theory which takes quality either as = intensive quantity, or as a means to quantity in general. The "higher pleasure" is here the pleasure which contains in itself most degrees of pleasure, or which contributes on the whole to the existence of a larger number of degrees of pleasure. Here the principle of the greatest amount of

[17] Speaking roughly and inaccurately, we may say they are of this quality as containing more or fewer degrees of somewhat, or as the result of more or fewer degrees, or (what comes to the same thing) as producing a qualitative result which is referred to more or fewer degrees; *e.g.*, a certain warmth is higher because containing more degrees of objective heat; a piece of work is

pleasure is adhered to; that is the top, and what approaches to it or contributes to it is nearer the top. But since the moral "higher" is here, as we see, the more pleasurable or the means to the more pleasurable, we come in the end to the amount, the quantity of pleasure without distinction of kind or quality; and having already seen that such an end is not a moral end, we get nothing from the phrases "higher" and "lower" unless it be confusion.

(2) The second view is that which distinguishes pleasures by their *mere* quality. The "higher" pleasure here is not the more intense pleasure; it is not the pleasure connected with the maximum of pleasure on the whole without distinction of kind. It is the preferable kind of pleasure (Mill, *Util.*, p. 12).

The first point to be noticed is that our theory gives up and abandons the greatest amount of pleasure principle. If you are to prefer a higher pleasure to a lower without reference to quantity— then there is an end altogether of the principle which puts the measure in the surplus of pleasure to the whole sentient creation. It is no use saying all pleasures are ends, only some are more ends. It is no use talking of "estimation" and "comparison" (Mill, pp. 12, 17). You have no standard to estimate by, no measure to make comparisons with. Given a certain small quantity of higher pleasure in collision with a certain large quantity of lower, how can you decide between them? To work the sum you must reduce the data to the same denomination. You must go to quantity or nothing; you decline to go to quantity and hence you cannot get any result. But if you refuse to work the sum, you abandon the greatest amount of pleasure principle.

There is no harm in doing that; but what else have we to go to? The higher pleasures? And what are the higher pleasures? We find higher pleasure means nothing but the pleasure which those who have experienced both it and others do as a fact choose in preference. Higher then, as we saw above, has no meaning at all unless we go to something *outside* pleasure, for we may not go to quantity of pleasure. But, if we go outside pleasure, not only

higher if it is the result of more skill; and A's skill stands higher than B's, if A produces a result which B cannot produce, and if the result must be referred to the amount of skill in the performer.

have we given up the greatest amount theory but we have thrown over Hedonism altogether.[18]

Let us drop the word higher then, as we must. The end is pleasures in order, as they are preferred by men who know them. The objection which at once arises (p. 14) is, Is there not any difference of opinion? Do not different men, and does not even the same man at different times, prefer different pleasures? What is the answer? It is not very intelligible, and is too long to quote (pp. 14, 15). What it comes to would appear, however, to be either Yes or No. Let us consider these alternatives one at a time.

(1) If we say "Yes, not only do different men prefer different pleasures but so does the same man at different times," then what basis have we left for a moral system? Merely this. Most men at most times do prefer one sort of pleasure to another; and from this we have to show that I ought to prefer one sort of pleasure to others at all times. We need not ask how the transition is to be made from what most men do to what I am to do. I think it can be made on no view of human nature, and I am quite sure it cannot be made on Mill's view. Supposing then that in Mill's mouth moral obligation had a meaning, yet there is no reason why it should attach itself to the average pleasures of the average man.

(2) And if we say No, if having accepted the Platonic doctrine that the judge of pleasures is he who knows them all, we go further and assert with Socrates that no man is willingly evil, that you cannot prefer bad to good, that, if you take the bad, it is because you never have known or now do not know the good, we

[18] Mill is unaware that he has done so because of the various senses in which he uses the word happiness. Happiness is (pp. 8, 10) simply identified with pleasure. Then (13, 14) appears the doctrine that happiness may exist without contentment, and (I suppose) contentment without happiness. We hear (13) that the "sense of dignity" is "part" of happiness, and (19) we see happiness means a desirable kind of life. It is a "concrete whole" with "parts" (55). It has "ingredients" (53) and appears to be a mere "aggregate" or "collective something." Instead of pleasure it has plainly come to mean something like the life we prefer, and hence greatest happiness will stand for the widest and intensest realization of such an ideal. This is to leave Hedonism altogether. [My references throughout are to *Utilitarianism*, 1st ed., the only one I have at hand.]

then I think are in good company, but in no better case. For an opponent will hold to the fact that he does knowingly prefer what is called bad to good, and will hence, by our argument, conclude first that bad is really good, and next that nothing can be either good or bad, since bad to one man is good to another. And if we, on the other hand, persist that the fact is impossible (I do not know how we are to prove it so), and that no one ever did or could choose what we call bad, when he had in his mind what we call good, then we identify immorality with ignorance and moral obligation disappears. For every man not only does, but must do, the best on every occasion so far as he knows it; his knowledge is an accident which has nothing to do with his will; he must act up to the ought, so far as he has an ought, and he cannot do what he thinks is wrong.

To proceed—the basis of our moral theory is now, There is a scale of pleasures; some persons know all, and others only some; but you necessarily choose the pleasures you know according to the scale. I, *e. g.*, know the alphabet of pleasures, always or sometimes, up to M. "Immoral man to choose M when you should have chosen P or R or even X." But I do not know what they are. "And therefore you are immoral for I and a good many other people do." But let us drop the matter here; on such a theory, the reader will assent, moral obligation is unmeaning.[19]

[19] At the risk of hypercriticism I will make one or two further remarks on Mill's view. According to it, pleasures must stand in a kind of order of merit, represented, let us say, by the letters of the alphabet. All pleasures, because pleasures, are good in themselves. A pleasure is immoral only when taken where a higher was possible, now or as a consequence. Then every pleasure is moral because it has a supposable pleasure below it; every pleasure is immoral because there is always a supposable pleasure above it. No man is moral because his knowledge is limited and he therefore cannot always take the highest conceivable pleasure; but if so, then all men are equally moral for they all take the highest pleasure they know. Or, passing by this, let us suppose the pleasures divided into two classes — higher and lower. If the lower are to be considered at all, then, as we have said, in the event of a collision the problem is insoluble because what is not of the same denomination cannot be compared. Let us suppose then that the lower are not to be considered and we are left with the higher. Here the same problem breaks out. For these pleasures are no system; if you make the idea

On either supposition, then, these preferable pleasures found
no "ought" in the moral sense—you have them or you have them
not, you like them or you do not like them, you know them or
you do not know them, and there is an end of it. If A, B, and
C call D immoral, D may return the epithet, and if he likes to say
"ignorance is morality" or to make any other assertion whatever,
he can do it, as it appears to me, on precisely the same ground as
A, B, and C have for their assertions, viz., no ground at all but
likes and dislikes.

And here I think we might leave the matter; but, having gone
so far, we may as well go a little further. Not only has moral
obligation nothing in Mr. Mill's theory to which it can attach
itself save the likes or dislikes of one or more individuals, but in
the end it *is* itself nothing more than a similar feeling.

"The ultimate sanction of all morality" is "a subjective feeling
in our minds" (p. 41), and the "moral faculty" is "susceptible
by a sufficient use of the external sanctions, and of the force of
early impressions of being cultivated in almost any direction; so

of a system your end, and regulate the pleasures by that, you have deserted
Hedonism. The pleasures are no system and they are not all of equal value.
Hence, as above, they cannot be calculated quantitatively. In the event of
collisions then (such as must take place) between *e.g.* the pleasures of
philosophy, pleasures of natural science, pleasures of virtue, pleasures of love,
pleasures of the table, pleasures of the "theopathic affections," pleasures of
fine art, pleasures of history, etc., you have again a problem which cannot be
solved except by the caprice of the individual who will prefer for himself and
others what he likes best.

Another point of interest is that the theory which begins with the most
intense democracy, wide enough to take in all life that feels pleasure and
pain, ends in a no less intense Platonic aristocracy. The higher pleasure is
to be preferred to any amount of the lower, and I suppose is to constitute the
moral standard. But clearly the beasts are incapable of refined pleasures;
the vulgar are better, but still very low; the only man who knows the highest
pleasure is the philosopher. He is moral, the universe below is immoral in
increasing degree. And, since no amount of lower can weigh against higher,
and, since the highest pleasures (and only the philosopher can judge what
they are, for only he knows all) are realizable only in the few, therefore we
must live for the few, and not for the many. And I suppose the same
argument might be used by the artist, or well-nigh anyone else. But it is
not worth while to pursue the matter further.

that there is hardly anything so absurd or so mischievous that it may not, by means of these influences, be made to act on the human mind with all the authority of conscience" (p. 44). The feeling of obligation then, we see, does not refer itself essentially to anything in particular. And further, "this sanction has no binding efficacy on those who do not possess the feelings it appeals to" (p. 42). "The sanction, so far as it is disinterested, is always in the mind itself, and the notion, therefore, of the transcendental moralists must be that this sanction will not exist *in* the mind, unless it is believed to have its roots out of the mind, and that, if a person is able to say to himself, This which is restraining me and which is called my conscience is only a feeling in my own mind, he may possibly draw the conclusion that when the feeling ceases the obligation ceases, and that, if he find the feeling inconvenient, he may disregard it and endeavor to get rid of it" (pp. 42, 43). This is a serious matter and I should say that any theory which maintains that a man may get rid of his sense of moral obligation if he can, and that, if he does so, the moral obligation is gone, is as grossly immoral a theory as ever was published. Does Mr. Mill repudiate the doctrine? Not at all; he evidently accepts it, though he prefers not to say so. The passage goes on: "But is this danger confined to the Utilitarian morality?" etc. Now I am ashamed of repeating it so often but I must entreat the reader not to have dust thrown in his eyes in this way, and not to be distracted by "transcendental moralis" or any other bugbears. The question is, Is theory A true, or are we obliged to say that either theory A is false or the facts are a lie? The question is not, Have theories B and C the same fault as A? When we have done with A we will then, if we choose, go to B and C; and if they turn out *all* false that does not prove *one* true. These pleader's devices are in place in a law court, but philosophy does not recognize them.

If then all that the moral "ought" means is that I happen to have a feeling which I need not have, and that this feeling attaches itself now to one set of pleasures and now to another set according to accident or my liking, would it not be better altogether to have done with the word, and, as some have done, openly to reject it and give it up since already we have given up all that it stands for? But if we give up the word then we have confessed that, as a theory of morals, Hedonism is bankrupt and we left with nothing but our "natural sentiment."

Hedonism *is* bankrupt. With weariness we have pursued it, so far as was necessary, through its various shapes—from the selfish doctrine of the individual to the self-sacrificing spirit of modern Utilitarianism. We have seen that in every form it gives an end which is illusory and impalpable. We have seen that its efforts to compromise with the moral consciousness are useless; that in no shape will it give us a creed that holds water, and that will justify to the inquiring mind those moral beliefs which it is not prepared for the sake of any theory to relinquish. Whatever we may think of those who embrace the doctrine, whatever may be its practical results, yet, theoretically considered, we have seen, I trust, that it is immoral and false, and are ready to endorse the saying, Ἡδονὴ τέλος, πόρνης δόγμα.

Modern Utilitarianism has a good object in view. Though we understand it differently, we have the same object in view, and that is why we are at issue with Utilitarianism.

We agree that it is desirable to have a standard of virtue which is palpable and "objective"; and therefore we refuse to place the end in what is most impalpable, what is absolutely and entirely "subjective."

We agree that the end is not the realization of an abstract idea; and therefore we refuse to take as our end the greatest amount of pleasure, for that is an abstract idea, and it is altogether unrealizable.

We agree that the end is not a "thing-in-itself," is not Heaven knows what or where, but is the end for us as men, τἀνθρώπινον ἀγαθόν; and therefore we refuse to find it in that element of the mind which is *least* distinctively human, and shared with us by the beasts that perish.

We agree that it must be κτητὸν ἀνθρώπῳ; and therefore we refuse to seek for it in that which has become a proverb for its fallaciousness.

We agree in the refusal to separate actions and consequences;

and therefore we refuse to abstract from action one moment, viz.,
the accompanying or the consequent feeling, and put our test in
the more or less of that.

We agree that happiness is the end; and therefore we say
pleasure is not the end.

We agree that pleasure is *a* good; we say it is not *the* good.

We agree (strange fellowship!) with the author of the *Essay on
Liberty* in affirming the ὃ πᾶσι δοκεῖ τοῦτ' εἶναι φαμέν; and therefore
we dissent from a theory which gives the lie to the moral consciousness and whose psychological basis destroys and makes unmeaning the maxim.

We agree to make the self-evolution of ourselves and of humanity the end. We refuse to place progress in the greater or less
amount of "grateful feeling." We repeat the good old doctrine that
the test of higher and lower cannot lie in a feeling which accompanies the exercise of every function, but is to be found in the
quality of the function itself. To measure that, we are to go to our
idea of man and to his place in creation and his evolution in
history.

In one single word, the end and the standard is self-realization,
and is not the feeling of self-realizedness.

May we suggest, in conclusion, that of all our Utilitarians there
is perhaps not one who has not still a great deal to learn from
Aristotle's *Ethics?*[20]

[20] Since the above was written Mr. Sidgwick's book has appeared. I am
far from wishing to deny to it a certain value, but on the subject of Hedonism
I cannot honestly say more than that he seems to me to have left the question
exactly where he found it. As other people, however, seem to think otherwise, I am forced to define my position against him. But I labor here under
two difficulties — the first, want of space; the second, my inability to make
sure of Mr. Sidgwick's meaning.

The latter arises in great measure from the character of the work. Ostensibly critical, it goes throughout upon preconceptions which not only are not
discussed but which often are not even made explicit. With some of these
we must begin.

(1) It is tacitly assumed that the individual and the universal are two
independent things (p. 473). Hence the *mere* individual is not (as with us)
an abstraction in our heads, but a real existence.

(2) The practical result of this dogmatic preconception is seen on p. 374.

To find a man's ultimate end we are to suppose "only a single sentient conscious being in the universe." This supposition *pre*supposes either that the universe is real out of relation to all consciousness, or is real in relation to one finite consciousness. An author no doubt has a right to maintain these or any other propositions, but whence he gets a right quietly to take them for granted I should be glad to be informed.

(3) But let us suppose the possibility of a finite subject alone in a material universe, and then let us look at Mr. Sidgwick's views from the ground of common sense.

On this ground I say (a) for myself, I cannot imagine myself into the position of this solitary sentient and doubt if the author, or anyone else, can do so. (b) Passing this by, we come to the assertion that such a supposed being would consider itself to have some rational end, some ultimate good, something right and reasonable as such, for which to live. All I can say here is that so far as I can imagine myself absolutely alone in a material world, I do not think it would occur to me that I had anything to live for. (c) Supposing however that, being forced so to continue, I did avoid pain and get pleasure, it would not occur to me to say that therefore I was realizing an "intrinsically and objectively desirable," the "end of Reason," the "absolutely Good or Desirable."

Surely common sense must see that, to find what end we ought to pursue in the human life we live, by seeing what would be left us to pursue in an unimaginable and inhuman predicament, is not common sense at all but simply bad metaphysics. No doubt a mere quantity is no more than the sum of its units, and to find the value of each unit no doubt you must isolate it by division. But tacitly to assume that the moral world is a mere sum of units whose value can be found separately, is really nothing but an enormous piece of dogmatism.

Starting from these preconceptions as to the nature of the individual, we have to get to the conclusion that the pleasure of all is the end for each, which problem we have seen above is insoluble. Mr. Sidgwick has an argument whereby he "suppresses Egoism," which, so far as I can take it in, is as follows:

(1) We *do*, as a fact, desire objects other than our pleasures. But
(2) Our private pleasure is for us the sole ultimate or rational desirable. But
(3) Our private pleasure as such is not rational. Therefore
(4) It is rational for us to desire something other than it. And because
(5) Pleasure is the only thing we *can desire* (?); therefore
(6) We desire, and are to desire, pleasure as rational. But that means pleasure in general, *i. e.*, pleasure without reference to any feeling subject in particular.

(This is, of course, not Mr. Sidgwick's statement, but my understanding, or very likely my misunderstanding, of him; so I shall not examine it in this form.)

He takes from Utilitarianism the pleasure of all as my end, whether I happen to want it or not. He takes from the popular interpretation of the moral consciousness the desire for "the right and reasonable as such." These seem to go well together, and we say, "I am to desire the pleasure of all as right and reasonable as such." This assertion being emphatically repudiated, it is necessary to prove it. How to do this? As before, isolate a man and you will see that he perceives intuitively that it is right and reasonable for him to pursue pleasure. This means that he perceives two things: (1) that he desires his private pleasure, (2) that he desires the reasonable. Put them together and you get the argument: (a) the reasonable is not my private pleasure, (b) other people's pleasure is not my private pleasure. Therefore (c) other people's pleasure is reasonable. Or, if this is not meant, perhaps the assertion is that the isolated man sees two things together, both that his pleasure is the reasonable end, and that not *his* pleasure, but pleasure as such, is so. In that case would it not be better to say at once, "I intuitively perceive that the Utilitarian conclusion is right"? for then the reply, "But I do not," would end the argument.

However Mr. Sidgwick may get to his conclusion, he has to make it good against two parties—(1) those who assert the right and reasonable, but deny that it is pleasure; (2) those who deny the right and reasonable, but assert pleasure as *my* private pleasure. (1) The first party (so far as I can represent them) have spoken already. We deny the intuition, and the reasoning we have sufficiently refuted by stating it; and if we wished to do more, we should do well to press for some further account of the phrases "objectively desirable," "real end of reason," etc. If my pleasure is my sole end, if the objective is (also) my end, then I should say there is a hopeless contradiction in which we stick. (2) But Mr. Sidgwick's attitude toward Egoism is more instructive. Having first (after Butler) rightly denied the basis of Hedonism, viz., the assertion that I desire nothing but pleasure, he throws himself repentant into the arms of the true faith, and says, "Though as a fact other things are or seem to be desired, yet nothing but my pleasure is *desirable*. My pleasure is the end." Here we have Egoism. "But," says Mr. Sidgwick, "the right and reasonable is objectively desirable." "Not so," replies the Egoist. "The *objectively* desirable is a fiction. The distinction of desir*ed* and desir*able* is wholly fallacious unless 'desirable' is a clumsy name for the means to what I desire. The end is what I do desire and that is just what I happen to like; 'reasonable' is what I correctly conclude is a means to that; and for 'right' and 'ought,' if they are not a misleading way of saying this over again, they are as nonsensical as 'objective end of reason.'" And against this Mr. Sidgwick, having left the only true line, has nothing to say but that he hopes the Egoist will be good enough to admit that something is objectively desirable as an end. If the Egoist does so, he is "suppressed" certainly, and deserves to be. But will he do so? I recommend the reader to peruse Stirner's book, *Der Einzige und sein Eigenthum*.

Mr. Sidgwick asserts that only my pleasure is desirable and that I desire this as objectively desirable. But (1) *If* I desire my pleasure as mine in particular, is it not a flat contradiction to say I desire it as *not* mine in particular? And (2) *can* I desire *my* pleasure *as* pleasure in general? Is not that a pure fiction invented to support a weak compromise — a fiction which neither of the parties opposed would, if they understood their position, attend to for a moment? Is my feeling pleased anything *but* my feeling pleased? Can you put the "feeling pleased" on the one side and the "my" on the other? I know but one theory on which this is possible and that is the view which, while it regards the distinctions of "me" and "you" as mere illusion or "Maja," nevertheless maintains that the pleasure and pain are not mere illusion. Against this view I am not called on to argue, and Mr. Sidgwick is, I imagine, no more a friend to it than I am.

I have criticized Mr. Sidgwick sharply, not from want of respect, but because I must be brief and fear to be obscure. Whether I understand him or not, I do not know; and with respect to what Mr. Bain has said on the same subject this again is my case. As to what he means by "disinterested action" I have not the least idea. He speaks of "entering into the feelings of another being," which, on his view, is to me much as if he said, "One bag of marbles enters into the marbles of another bag"; and again (*Emotions*, etc., 3rd ed., p. 267), he talks of "pleasures whose nature is to take in other sentient beings," which, again, is as if he said, "There are some marbles whose nature it is to take in other bags of marbles." Either these things are illusions or not. If they are not, it seems to me they revolutionize the whole of Mr. Bain's psychology. If they are, I want to know whether and why we are to rest our Ethics upon them. What seems clear to me is this—Pleasure is the one end or it is not. If it is not, then Hedonism goes. If it is, then *my* pleasure is my end. The pleasure of others is neither a feeling in me nor an idea of a feeling in me. If it seems to be so, this is a mere illusion. If what is not my feeling or its idea is my end, then the root of Hedonism is torn up. If so, the argument from the individual to the race disappears because pleasure is *not* the sole end of the individual.

In this plight, nothing is left to Hedonism but an appeal to the facts of society. If these show that progress so far involves increase of pleasure (and here, on the question of fact, Hedonism has to meet Pessimism), that does not prove it will be always so; still less does it prove that the idea of increase of pleasure *is* the moving cause of progress, and even less that it *ought* to be.

NOTE

There are two questions suggested by the above—(1) Is pleasure good, and if so, in what sense is it good? (2) Is pain evil and in what way is it evil? Let us take the latter first.

Considered psychically pain is an evil because it is the feeling of the negation of the self or life. The good is the affirmation of the self and hence pain is counter to the good. If we are asked to suppose a pain which is a feeling of negation, but not a felt negation, i. e., which is not really in any way the negation of function or the cause of such negation, and are then asked, Is such hypothetical pain an evil? we cannot say it would be, because we can say nothing about it at all. It seems to us to be an unreal abstraction. Real pain is the feeling of the negatedness of the self and therefore, as such, it is bad. It is bad also because it further acts in the direction of the general lowering of life. Both as felt diminution of the good and as the cause of further diminution, it is an evil.

If, where pain comes from negated function, but the function is supposed to be indifferent, we are asked, Is then the pain bad? we reply that it is so because the whole self is negated—*I* feel pain, and am therein lowered directly or indirectly.

In passing we may ask, Is then pain on the whole an evil? We cannot say that. We know that pain often is a good; and we should have a right to say of any pain that it was an absolute evil only if we knew that it was pain *per se, i. e.*, mere negation. But that is what we cannot know. Speaking generally, you cannot have mere pain, the negative without the positive; painlessness means death; pain appears to involve reaction; and again, wherever there is an active conscious self it seems there must be pain. To say that pain is an absolute evil we should have to answer in the affirmative the question, Can you have the positive without the negative, or the negative in this form? And I do not see how we can give this answer. We know that pain is often a stimulus; without some pain little is produced—perhaps nothing. We know

that the pain of the part is often the good of the whole; that the
good demands sometimes even the destruction of the part. The
life of the whole is the end and for this all must be sacrificed. And
so the question is, Is the negation of the part always a condition
of the affirmation of the whole, or is it sometimes not? (And we
should remember that the affirmation of the whole may be in the
part or without the part.) Can we ever say, Here is an overplus
of the negative; here is negation of function, which, in itself and
its results, is negation of the good, or of life as a whole? I do
not see how we are to say this because I do not see how we can
know enough about the whole of things. For anything I can tell
pain *per se* may be always an unreal abstraction, as I know it
often is. What is bad for this or that relative totality may be
good for a higher; and above the highest relative totality may be
(for anything I know to the contrary) an absolute totality in
which and for which pain is the mere condition of affirmation
and in no sense the diminution of life, but whose life (as I suppose all life) involves in itself a subordinated negation. This I
do not assert to be the case; but I wished to point out that no man
has a right to say pain is an evil absolutely unless he knows that
there is no such life of the whole, or that pain is a negative which
limits its functions, and is not a negative condition of those
functions.

To return from our digression. We have seen that pain is bad
whenever it is not necessary as a condition of good. Turning
now to pleasure, we ask, Is pleasure, generally speaking, good?
Doubtless it is good. It is the felt assertion of the will or self.
It is felt self-realizedness. It is good because it accompanies and
makes a whole with good activity, because it goes with that self-
realization which is good; or secondly, because it heightens the
general assertion of self, which is the condition of realizing the
good in self.

Pleasure is the physical accompaniment of exercise of function
and a distinction is required in order to think of function apart
from some pleasure. Perhaps there is really no such thing. The
function brings its own pleasure, however small, though the whole
state may be painful.

Pleasure, then, is generally good; but the questions which now arise are, Can pleasure exist without function? If so, is it good? Or to put it otherwise, Are all pleasures of activity good? Are all pleasures of passivity good? Are any pleasures neither good nor bad? And finally, Is any pleasure good *per se,* or simply as pleasure?

Can pleasure exist without function? We could not enter here on a psychological investigation of the point even were we able to treat the matter satisfactorily. But taking pleasure to be the feeling of the realizedness of the will or self, we should doubt if apart from some present function or activity pleasure could exist. The questions to be answered would be, how far in what seem the most, or mere, "passive pleasures" of sense function is concerned; how far in contemplative pleasures activity of contemplation comes in; how far, lastly, the very feeling of self, which is pleasure, in being felt implies an activity. To a tired man, for instance, the pleasure of lying down in bed is great; he wants no more; it is complete affirmation of his will, perfect satisfiedness. But as he grows more and more sleepy does his pleasure increase? When he is asleep does he feel pleasure? On the other hand, is he less satisfied? and if so, in what sense? If his pleasure has been diminished or has ceased, is not that because the reaction, the function of the feeling center has ceased or been diminished; and is not that reaction what is felt when pleasure is felt?

Let us, however, pass by this question, as without answering it decidedly we hope to show how far pleasure is good. Roughly speaking, we can distinguish pleasures of activity and passivity; pleasure which comes with our doing something, and pleasure which we do nothing to get.[1] Let us ask with each class when pleasure is good and when it is bad, if it is bad.

(1) We will first take pleasures of activity.

(*a*) When are they good? When the activity is good the pleasure is good because the two are a physical whole. You cannot have the function without the pleasure—the absence of the

---

[1] We need not distinguish further the pleasure of having something done to us. It will, I think, be covered by our answer, and it is a somewhat complicated state of mind.

pleasure would weaken and perhaps destroy the function, and also generally lower the self to the detriment of other functions; whereas presence of pleasure tends to the heightening of functions in general, besides its own function. Then what activities are good? Detail is impossible but, generally, those which directly realize the good will in a living man, or which indirectly increase life and so the possibility of a higher realization of the good in a living man or men. Or rather the two cannot be divided. Life is a whole; and life is not only the condition of the good but may be taken as another name for it. "The end of life is life," and (speaking generally) what heightens life heightens the good. Pleasure then is not a means to the good but is included in it and belongs to it.

(b) What pleasures of activity are bad then? for admittedly there are such. The pleasure is bad when the activity is bad, and the activity is bad when, in its immediate or ulterior results, it lowers the life of the individual or of a larger totality, and so diminishes realization of good, or prevents a higher and fuller realization. Here pleasure is bad because it strengthens and intensifies a bad activity. The pleasure *per se* is not bad, but then there is no such thing except in our heads.

(2) Next as to pleasures of passivity. Let us for shortness' sake exclude artistic pleasures, and take pleasures of sensuous satisfaction. Are passive sensuous pleasures good or bad? In themselves, I think, they are neither good nor bad. Or we may say roughly, they are good when they are not bad.

(a) When are they bad? This is not hard to answer. They are bad when they prevent or retard the realization of the good life in us by preventing action. This they do when they produce special results which hinder the good, or when they generally contribute toward a habit of self-indulgence, which is bad because it retards or opposes the activity of the good. In short, they are bad when they lower life or prevent its progress. They are not bad *per se*, but then here again they do not exist *per se*.

(b) When are they good? They are good when (without the evil results just mentioned) they increase what is ordinarily called happiness, a feeling of general content with one's existence. That is good because existence is good, and because without happiness existence is impaired, and with it the good; and because happiness (generally speaking) increases activity. Discontent and unhappiness are great evils, for (even if they do not lead to immorality) they lower life and activity for good. "Life is the end of life," and so what makes life more liveable is good; and life further must be realized in living men, the basis of whose nature is and must remain animal. To neglect the basis is to make as great a mistake as to regard it as the crown and summit. Life is a whole; and hence pleasures inseparable from life, and pleasures that maintain and heighten a feeling of well-being and joy in living (which again heightens life), are good because life is good—supposing, that is, that they are not bad, in the sense described above.

We come now to the two questions—Are any pleasures neither good nor bad? Are any pleasures good *per se?*

(1) Are any pleasures neither good nor bad? The ordinary man would say Yes. A certain amount of pleasure is undeniably good; and (as a rule), if you want more, the more is good (where it is not bad), and this because the satisfaction of the want is good for you, or the nonsatisfaction bad. Then again undeniably there is (speaking generally) a too much of any particular pleasure and that too much is bad. But between enough and too much, as in the pleasures of eating and drinking, there comes a neutral territory. It is probably good for you to have say not less than two glasses of wine after dinner. Six on ordinary occasions is perhaps too many; but, as to three or four, they are neither one way nor the other. If asked, is the pleasure of these intermediates bad? we say No. If asked, is it good? I do not think we can say Yes. If asked, is it not a positive addition to the surplus of pleasure? I do not think we can say No. We should put the whole question aside as idle. We should say the pleasure is neither good nor bad, or at least we do not know that it is. So far the ordinary man.

Now whether this margin is scientifically defensible, whether there must not be a point say of number of drops or fractions of

drops which is good, and beyond which acme you fall at onc
into badness, we shall not discuss. It is not an easy questio
and fortunately the answer matters nothing to our argument. Bu
for the ordinary man clearly some pleasures are neither good no
bad, and this because (for him) they do neither harm nor good

(2) To come now to the question, Is any pleasure a good *pe
se?* we are in a position, I think, to answer it in the negative
Ordinarily it does sound absurd to say mere pleasure is not an
end since at first sight it seems desirable. The foregoing, how
ever, should have removed this difficulty. We have seen that th
pleasures pronounced desirable are so because they are inseparabl
from and heighten life; and hence these pleasures are not pleasure
per se. And further, if the doctrine of the indifferent margin wer
indefensible (we believe that it is not so), then *no* pleasure coul
be a pleasure *per se,* and our present question would disappear

But supposing that there exist pleasures which are only pleasu
able and, so to speak, end in themselves, then these may certainl
be desired, but I think they are not considered desirable or good
And, if that is so, then, in denying that pleasure in itself is good
we are not in collision with the ordinary consciousness. To illus
trate: Having had three glasses of wine I may say I think so muc
was desirable. I certainly may have another if I like, and
suppose it will give me a certain amount of pleasure and no pai
or lessening of pleasure, now or afterwards. Is the surplus good
Is it desirable? Clearly, though a pleasure, and though not bad
it may not be good; and such is the case, I think, with a
innocent pleasures, as *e. g.* those of physical exercise, sports an
games, sight-seeing, etc. If this be so, however, then common con
sciousness does *not* hold pleasure *per se* to be desirable or goo
And as for philosophical arguments, what and where are they

We have now seen that pleasure is good so far as inseparabl
from life, and so far as it results in the heightening of life. Bu
in itself, if and so far as we separate it by an abstraction or find
apart from its good qualities, it is not good, it is in no sense a
end in itself.

Here we might cease, but further elucidations will perhaps nc
be superfluous.

Life is an end in itself. It is true that life implies pleasure. Pessimism notwithstanding, it implies, speaking generally, a surplus of pleasure; and I am not called upon to deny (though I certainly neither assert nor admit it) that higher life means always a greater surplus.

If so, have we come back to Hedonism? Since pleasure and life are inseparable, can we say that to aim at the realization of life is to aim at pleasure? No, in the sense of making it an object it is not to aim at pleasure; and this distinction is a vital difference which we must never slur. Function carries pleasure with it as its physical accompaniment, but what determines, makes, and is good or bad, is in the end function. Function, moreover, is something comparatively definite. It gives something you can aim at, something you can do. Not so the pleasure. Further, so far as function and pleasure are separable objects of choice, we must, if we are moral, choose the former. If they are inseparable, are one whole, why are we to aim at the indefinite side, at the subjective psychical sequent and accompaniment when we have an objective act which we can see before us and perform, and which is the prius of the feeling? It is the act carries with it the pleasure, not the pleasure the act.

"Yes, but," it will be said, "we want *more* pleasure, more than we get with present function; and we will alter the function to get the pleasure." Then you must take one of these three positions. You (a) wholly reject the idea that one function is in itself higher than another; or, while believing in higher and lower functions, you say (b) pleasure is separable, or (c) inseparable from the higher.

On the first supposition (a) you break at once with common morality which does not believe that lower and higher stand for mere means to less or more pleasure. And (b) on the second you are confessedly immoral for, while believing in a higher, you propose to sacrifice it to pleasure. "Let us have pleasure, even at the cost of function," is not a moral point of view.[2]

---

[2] Nor can you reconcile yourself to common morality by saying, "But we will *only* increase the pleasure." For (1) either the increase of pleasure does

Thirdly (c) if you maintain more pleasure and higher function to be on the whole inseparable, you may at once be challenged as to the truth of that assertion; and if you are not allowed to assume it, you cannot assume that more pleasure is an end.

But allowing you for the present to assume that higher function and more pleasure go together, so that to have one is to have the other, why (I would ask), if these two are one whole, will you persist in isolating one side of that whole since surely it is the less knowable side? The coincidence of the two is an extremely general truth; it need not be true for this man or generation; and, if so, how is it possible to aim at progress except by aiming at function? The function must (on the whole and in the end) carry the pleasure with it, and it is surely a more definite mark. Is it not preposterous to think of aiming at more pleasure, in the end and on the whole (not in any future that we can see), in order, by making this the end, to get along with it some higher function which we know nothing about? Is it not (e. g.) hopelessly vague, if we want to find out what the divine will is to attempt to define it by some idea of pleasure in the end and on the whole, and not to ourselves or any one else in any time that we can see? Is it not less vague to study that will by considering the previous evolution of it, and to accept what seems a higher step in that evolution as an end in itself? Must we not say that this going together of function and pleasure is a mere general faith which we cannot verify by experience in every case, and so cannot use to determine our particular course?

Of course one sees quite clearly that, generally speaking, it is a good thing to aim at the increasing of pleasure and diminishing of pain; but it is a good thing because it increases the actuality and possibilities of life. To make function the end justifies and demands the increase of pleasure and gives you all you can fairly ask in that way. But to say more pleasure is all the end, and life a mere accompaniment to that, is another matter.

And again, when we are doubtful what is higher in progress

issue in the heightening of function, and will be good in this sense and not in yours; or else (2), as we have seen, if pleasure neither raises nor lowers function, then common opinion considers it neither desirable nor undesirable it may be a safe course to increase pleasure and diminish pain because that heightens the good functions we have. But to look on the increase of pleasure as the mark to aim at always and simply, when we aim at progress, is again a very different course.

But, leaving this subject, we must observe that we have no right to assume that higher function and more pleasure do on the whole go together. We have bitter proof that in particular cases and stages of progress this is not the case, and so are forced to separate the two in our minds. We can *imagine* function without pleasure since we have experienced decrease of pleasure proportionate to heightening of quality of function. But, when the two come thus before the mind separately, we feel we must choose function and not pleasure.

In conclusion, there is one way in which pleasure may be used as a test of function. It shows whether function is impeded in discharge or not. But by it you cannot tell higher from lower function; and, if you go by it you must prefer a lower state of harmony to a higher state of self-contradiction.

For the sake of clearness I have run the risk of wearisome length and repetition. In the foregoing Essay I have sharply, not I hope too sharply, criticized Hedonism. From a somewhat more positive consideration I have reached the same result. And now in a spirit of conciliation I would ask the Utilitarian, whose heart is in the right place, who does not care about pleasure, but who wants something definite, to consider this—whether to take life as the end, the highest and ever a higher life, be *more* vague than Hedonism; whether it does not give him all he wants; and whether, beside being more in harmony with morality, it is not equally antagonistic to Asceticism.

If our end is to realize the life or the self which is realized in all life and to develop this in more distinctively human forms, and if we consider that this life to be realized *must* be realized in living individuals, we shall be far enough from asceticism. There is here no abstract negation of human nature, no sacrifice of detail and fullness to a barren formula. The universal is realized only in the free self-development of the individual, and the individual can only truly develop his individuality by specifying in himself the common life of all. As we repudiate the liberty of Individualism (better, Particularism), so we repudiate the tyranny of the (abstract) universal. The member is no member but a parasitical excrescence if it does not live with the life of the whole; the whole life does not exist except in the life of the members. And here, in the moral sphere, the members are self-conscious. It is then only in the intensity of the self-consciousness of the members that the whole can be intensely realized. Furthermore, these members are spiritualized animals; everything human stands on the basis of animal life; and to make self-realization the end not only justifies but demands attention to the well-being and happiness of man as a spiritualized animal, because the feeling of inner harmony is required for, is the psychical condition of, maintenance and progress of function. So far as this we go and must go, but no further; we ought not to sacrifice what seems to be maintenance or progress of function to prospect of increased pleasure. But I do not think that the Utilitarian *wishes* to teach that doctrine; and whatever he wants to teach he can teach without making pleasure the end. To repeat it once more, if self-realization is the end, then pleasure is a relative end and good, because a condition without which good is impossible; and hence to increase pleasure is good, though we need not add "for pleasure's sake." And unhappiness is evil if it is a psychical state which tends to exclude the good, and may be treated as an evil, which it is our bounden duty to fight against, without our being forced to say "it is the evil itself and there is no evil beyond it."

If again it is objected that the end is vague and has no content, the following Essays will to a certain extent, I hope, remove the objection. Here we may reply that to take human progress as the end, and to keep our eye on past progress, is not a useless prescription; and if any one wants a moral philosophy to tell him what in particular he is to do, he will find that there neither is nor can be such a thing, and at all events will not find it in Hedonism.

One word on the unconscious or latent Hedonism of society in its progress. That is no argument for making pleasure the end, as the reader who has followed me so far will, I trust, at once see. Taking for granted the asserted fact that society tends to identify what brings pleasure with what is good, we altogether deny the Hedonistic inference. If society tends to realize life more highly and perfectly, it is obvious that it must also realize the conditions of such life. The fact that life cannot exist without pleasure does not prove pleasure to be the end of life, unless we are prepared to say (the illustration is not a good one) that *because* as a man rises in society he wears better clothes, *therefore*, to be dressed like a gentleman was the conscious or unconscious end of his advancement. Of course, it might have been; but do we say that it was? Or, again, a mother *may* have desired her daughter's health not for her health's sake, but for the sake of her looks; but would it not be an unfounded inference to conclude that it *must* have been so? The argument we have noticed holds against asceticism, but we must entreat the reader to bear in mind that the opposite of a false view may be every whit *as* false; and that you could argue from the denial of asceticism to the assertion of Hedonism only if you had previously made good your alternative, your "either—or" of the two.

Finally (as we have already gone beyond all bounds), let us make a remark on the phrase "Utilitarianism." It is a thoroughly bad name and misleads a great many persons. It does indeed express the fact that, for Hedonism, virtue and action are *not* the end but are useful as mere means to something outside them. But surely it would be better to call the theory after its end (as we have done),[3] since to not a few persons "Utilitarianism" conveys the notion that the end is the useful, which, besides being strictly speaking sheer nonsense, is also misleading. The associations of the useful are transferred to Hedonism, and if these are in some ways unfavorable (Mill's *Util.*, p. 9), they seem to me in other and more ways to be favorable. The practical man hears of "the useful" and thinks he has got something solid, while he really is embracing (as I have shown) the cloud of a wild theoretical fiction from which he would shrink if he saw it apart from its false lights and colors. And on whichever side the balance of advantage lies, no respectable writer

[3] Since Mr. Sidgwick's book has appeared this has grown more common, and is a step in the right direction.

can wish to rest on a basis of misunderstanding. The two words "useful" and "happiness" delude not only the public but perhaps all Utilitarian writers. While they are the terms employed, the question cannot possibly be brought to a clear issue; and let me say for myself that I see no good reason why "Utilitarianism" should stand for Hedonism. If "happiness" means well-being or perfection of life, then I am content to say that, with Plato and Aristotle, I hold happiness to be the end; and, although virtue is not a *mere* means, yet it can be regarded as a means and so is "useful." In this sense we, who reject Hedonism, can call ourselves Utilitarians, and the man who thinks he is pushing some counterview by emphasizing "happiness" and "usefulness" does not touch us with his phrases, but rather perhaps confirms us. But pleasure for pleasure's sake, and life and virtue for the sake of pleasure, is another doctrine which we repudiate.

DUTY FOR DUTY'S SAKE

IN our answer to the question, Why should I be moral? we found that, explicitly or by implication, all Ethics pre-supposed something which is the good, and that this good (whatever else may be its nature) has always the character of an end. The moral good is an end in itself, is to be pursued for its own sake. It must not be made a means to something not itself. We have now seen further that pleasure is not the good, is not the end; that, in pursuing pleasure as such, we do not pursue the good. Hedonism we have dismissed and may banish it, if we please, from our sight, while we turn to develop a new view of the good, another answer to the question, What is the end? In Hedonism we have criticized a one-sided view; we shall have to do here with an opposite extremity of one-sidedness. The self to be realized before was the self or selves as a maximum quantity or number of particular feelings. In the theory which awaits us, the self to be realized has a defect which is diametrically opposed to the first, and yet is the same defect. Its fault is the opposite, since for mere particular it substitutes mere universal; we have not to do with feelings, as this and that, but with a form which is thought of as not this or that. Its fault is the same fault—the failing to see things as a whole, and the fixing as real one element which yet is unreal when apart from the other. In a word, we find in both a one-sided view, and their common vice may be called abstractness. So much by way of anticipation; and now we must betake ourselves to our task.

What is the moral end?[1] We know already in part what it is not. It is not a state or collection of states of the self, as feeling pleasure, to be produced either in me or outside me. To know

[1] What follows, the reader must be warned, is very far from being meant to be a statement of Kant's main ethical view; as such it would be neither complete nor accurate, though it will be found to be an applicable criticism. We could not give a statement of Kant's view without giving all the sides of it; and, were we prepared to do that, not only would considerable

81

what it *is* we must go to the moral consciousness. We find there that the end is for me as active, is a practical end. It is not something merely to be felt, it is something to be done.

And it is not something to be done, in which, when done, the doer is not to be involved. The end does not fall outside the doer. I am to realize myself; and, as we saw, I cannot make an ultimate end of anything except myself, cannot make myself a mere means to something else. Nor, again, does the end fall outside the activity. If the production in me of a mere passive state were the end, the activity would be a mere means to that. But the moral consciousness assures us that the activity is an end in itself. The end is a doing which is to be done; the activity is good in itself, not for the sake of a result beyond. The end, then, is not to be felt, but is to be done; it is to be done and not made; it falls not outside the self of the doer, nor further outside his activity.

In short, the good is the Good Will. The end is will for the sake of will; and, in its relation to me, it is the realization of the good will in myself, or of myself as the good will. In this character I am an end to myself, and I am an absolute and ultimate end. There is nothing which is good unless it be a good will.

This is no metaphysical fiction. It is the truth of life and of the moral consciousness. A man is not called good because he is rich, nor because he is handsome or clever. He is good when he is moral, and he is moral when his actions are conformed to and embody a good will, or when his will is good.

But "good will" tells us little or nothing. It says only *that* will is the end. It does not say *what* will is the end; and we want to know what the good will is.

What is the good will? We may call it indifferently the free will or the universal will, or the autonomous will, or finally the formal will.

space be required, but also we should be obliged to consider topics which lie outside our present undertaking. We have stated a view for purposes of criticism, but that criticism is at the same time a criticism that holds against more than our statement.

(1) It is the universal will. The very notion of the moral end is that it should be an end absolutely, not conditionally. It is not an end for me without being one also for you, or for you and me and not for a third person; but it is, without limitation to any this or that, an end for us all. And so the will, as end, is not the particular will of particular men, existing as this, that, and the other series of states of mind. It is the same for you and me and in the character of our common standard and aim it is above you and me. It is thus objective and universal.

(2) It is the free will. It is not conditioned by, it does not owe its existence and attributes to, it is not made what it is by, and hence it cannot (properly speaking) be called forth by, anything which is not itself. It exists because of itself and for the sake of itself. It has no end or aim beyond itself, is not constituted or determined by anything else.

Hence we see it is not determined by anything in particular. For, as we saw, it was universal, and universal means not particular; and so no more than a verbal conclusion is wanted to show that, if determined by something particular, it would be determined by something not itself. And this we have already taken to be false.

(3) It is autonomous. For it is universal and an end to itself. The good will is the will which wills the universal as itself and itself as the universal, and hence may be said to be a law to itself and to will its own law. And, because it is universal, hence in willing what is valid for itself it wills what is valid for all. It legislates universally in legislating for itself, since it would not legislate for itself did it not legislate universally.

(4) And lastly, it is formal. For, in willing itself, it wills the universal, and that is not-particular. Any possible object of desire, any wished-for event, any end in the shape of a result to be attained in the particular existence of myself or another, all are this or that something—they have a content, they are "material." Only that will is good which wills itself as not-particular, as without content or matter, in a word, which wills itself as form.

The good will, then, is the will which is determined by the form only, which realizes itself as the bare form of the will.

And this formal will is now seen to be the true expression for all the foregoing characteristics of universality, freedom, and autonomy. In formality we see they are all one. I am autonomous only because I am free, free only because I am universal, universal only because not particular, and not particular only when formal.

That the good must be formal we might have seen by considering its character of an universal standard or test. Such a standard is a form or it is nothing. It is to be above every possible this and that, and hence cannot be any this or that. It is by being *not* this or that, that it succeeds in having nothing which is not common to every this and that. Otherwise there would be something which would fall without its sphere; it would be only one thing among others, and so would no longer be a standard. But that which can be common to everything is not matter or content, but form only. As no material test of truth, so no material test of morality is possible.

The good will, then, is the bare form of the will, and this is the end. This is what I have to realize, and realize in myself. But I am not a mere form; I have an "empirical" nature, a series of particular states of the "this me," a mass of desires, aversions, inclinations, passions, pleasures, and pains, what we may call a sensuous self. It is in this self that all content, all matter, all possible filling of the form must be sought; for all matter must come from "experience," must be given in and through the perception of the outer world or of the series of my own internal states, and is in either case sensuous and the opposite of the insensible form.

The "empirical" self, the this me, is, no less than the self which is formal will, an element of the moral subject. These elements are antithetical the one to the other; and hence the realization of the form is possible only through an antagonism, an opposition which has to be overcome. It is this conflict and this victory in which the essence of morality lies. Morality is the activity of the formal self forcing the sensuous self, and here first can we attach a meaning to the words "ought" and "duty."[2]

---

[2] In a lower sense we can use, and do use, "ought" outside the moral world.

If our self were nothing beyond the series of its states, if it were nothing above and beyond these coexistent and successive phenomena, then the word "ought" could have no meaning. And again, if our self were a pure, unalloyed will, realizing itself apart from a sensuous element, the word "ought" would still be meaningless. It is the antagonism of the two elements in one subject which is the essence of the ought. The ought is a command; it expresses something which neither simply is or is not, but which both is and is not—something, in short, which is to be. Further, when addressed to myself, it puts before me something which is to be done and which I am to do. A command is the doing of something by me, which doing is willed by a will, not me, and presented as such by that will to me.[3] In the ought the self is commanded and that self is the sensuous self in me, which is ordered, and which, if I obey, is forced by the nonsensuous formal will which stands above the empirical element, and, equally with that, is myself. The ought is the command of the formal will, and duty is the obedience or, more properly, the compulsion of the lower self by that will, or the realization of the form in and against the recalcitrant matter of the desires.

Duty must be for duty's sake, or it is not duty. It is not enough that my acts should realize and embody the universal form, and so far be conformable thereto. It is not enough that the act commanded be done by me. The end, as we have seen, is not a result beyond and outside the activity. It is not the realizedness of the form which is the good, but rather the realization of it, because only as active is it negative, only as negative is it real.

Wherever "law" has a meaning, "ought" has also a meaning. Where the particular phenomenon does not answer to its conception, we say "ought." "A man (e. g.) 'ought' to have two eyes." "Ice of that thickness 'ought' to have borne." Something has interfered in the case so that the fact is not an exhibition of the law. But the moral "ought" means much more than this. There the particular fact or phenomenon is this or that *will*, which, moreover, is or can be *aware of its position* as such in relation to the law or general conception. This makes an enormous difference.

[3] A command *may* contain a promise or threat. It is not of its essence that it should do so.

And further, the good is not merely the realization of the form by a foreign subject, but its own realization of itself by itself. That does not take place unless the act ordered to be done in the field of the lower self is done by me in the character of the formal self. If that is so, I must know that it is so; and if I do not know that it is so, then it is not so. Duty is not duty unless, in every case and in every act, it is consciously done for the sake of duty, and that means for the sake of the realization of the bare form, and of nothing whatever beside the bare form. And hence we see that an act done from pleasure in or desire for the bare form can in no case be dutiful; for that would be the lower nature, for some liking of its own, choosing to realize the form; it could not be the form realizing itself; and hence such an act is not in any degree moral, since in no degree does it attain the end. The lower self in morality is not led, nor coaxed, nor consulted, but forced.

Here again we appeal to the moral consciousness to bear testimony to our conclusion. Every moral man knows that to do right is to do one's duty for its own sake, and that, if duty is done for the sake of some ulterior object, that act may be legal but is certainly not moral.

Having found ourselves in accord with practical morality, and resting on the conclusion that no act is moral except that which is consciously done for the sake of the universal form, we have now to state the rule which is to guide our practice in life and which is too simple to occasion any trouble in the working. We have to realize the good will, the will that is an end in itself, and that is universally valid; and, as we saw, these characteristics are summed up in formality. The standard, we saw, must be formal; it must exclude all possible content because content is diversity; and hence the residue left to us for a standard is plainly identity, the identity which excludes diversity; and of this we can say only that it is, and that it does not contradict itself. Our practical maxim, then, is, Realize noncontradiction. Realize, *i.e.*, act and keep acting; do not contradict yourself, *i.e.*, let all your acts embody and realize the principle of noncontradiction; for so only can you realize the formal will which is the good will. Whatever act embodies a self-contradiction is immoral. Whatever act is self-consistent is legal. Whatever act is self-consistent and is done for the sake of realizing self-consistency, and for the sake of nothing else, is moral. This is simple, this is practical; and there surely is cause for thankfulness in the arrangement of things which has placed the standard and test of all that is most important, of everything which really is important, in a form which even the unlettered can understand and a child can apply.

Stated[4] as we have stated above, the theory of duty for duty's sake carries with it little or no plausibility. Criticism of it may appear to the reader to be superfluous, but nevertheless it will repay us to see briefly set forth the inner contradictions in which it loses itself, and which destroy its claim to practical value.

The theory contradicts itself and, reduced to a simple form, the contradiction is as follows: self-realization is the end, and the self to be realized is the negative of reality; we are to realize, and must produce nothing real. Let us explain. The good is the will. The will is the carrying of the inner mind out into the world of fact; it is the identity of thought and existence, the process in which the ideal passes over into reality, and where the content on both sides is the same, subject always to the diversity of the two different elements. Mere thought is not will—that is the inner side only. Mere existence in time and space, or time, is not will—that is the outside only. For will we want both sides, and both sides in one. And from the above we see at once that, if the two sides are to correspond, there must be some correspondence in the nature of what they contain; and, starting here from the side of existence, we may say, you can realize nothing unless that which you are to realize have in it already the character which distinguishes reality.

To realize means to translate an ideal content into existence, whether it be the existence of a series of events in time only, as

---

[4] As I said before, this is not a statement of the Kantian view; that view is far wider, and at the same time more confused. As a system it has been annihilated by Hegel's criticism (I, 335, ff.; and II, 437, ff.), to which I owe most of the following. Compare also Schopenhauer, *Die beiden Grund-probleme der Ethik* (1881), 117-178. But the reader must bear in mind that only I am responsible for what I say.

in mere psychical acts, or existence both in space and time, as is the case in all outward acts.[5]

Neither to give a proper definition of the real, nor to discuss the nature of existence in space and time, and its relation to thought in general, and in particular to human thought, even were I competent to do it, would be possible here. But I do not suppose I shall find much contradiction if I say that the predominant character of existence in space and time is, in one word, its particularness, what is ordinarily called its concreteness, the infinitude of its relations. An existing thing and the mere thought of a thing are not the same, if that be taken to mean that there is no difference between them; and, especially in morals, the distance between theory and fact is as immeasurable as the distance between what is thought and what is willed, between a definition and the thing defined. As I have said before, we cannot go into these fundamental questions, but so much seems clear—that, as against a theory, definition, or abstract principle, the main character of existence in space and time is the endless detail of its particular relations. You cannot particularize a definition so as to exhaust any sensible object, since that object stands in relation to every other thing in the world.

Let us say then that to realize (whatever else it is beside) is at least to particularize, and we shall see how the theory of duty for duty's sake contradicts itself. (1) It says you are not to do what it says you are to do; what you have to effect is the negation of the particular; and so it says in a breath, realize and do not realize. (2) It gives you no content; and that which has no content cannot be willed since in volition we must have the same content on each side. (3) Psychically considered, an act of will is a particular act and hence a formal act of will is impossible.

To explain: (1) You are to realize the good will and that means the formal will, or the universal will. But universal means the

---

[5] This is true of course only so long as psychical events are considered simply as such. Every psychical state *has* also, I suppose, its existence in space. In this connection let me add in passing, that whether the will has *direct* control over the thoughts or not is an open question in psychology. It is indifferent to us here what answer be given.

opposite of particular. "Realize the particular" means, realize the
opposite of the universal; and so, if you particularize the universal,
you have not realized *it*, *i. e.*, not the universal you had to realize;
or, in other words, if you materialize the form, it is no longer
formal. On the other hand, "realize" *means* materialize, it *means*
particularize. "Realize" *asserts* the concrete identity of matter
and form which "formal will" denies; and we are left with the
hopeless contradiction of an order, which tells us in one breath
that only the formal (*i. e.*, the *not*-real) will is good, and that for
the sake of the good we are to realize (*i. e.*, unformalize) the
formal will.

Or less abstractly, we have two elements in one subject—the
sensuous nature and the pure will. The pure will is to be kept
pure; it is for its sake that we act, and action consists in the
forcing of the sensuous nature. The order is here, "Realize
the pure will in the sensuous nature," and the contradiction is as
above. The pure will means the nonsensuous will, and "realize
it" means translate it into an element which destroys its essence.
The formal will when realized is no longer formal, is materialized, is sensualized, is no longer pure. If you do not want
to sensualize the will, why do you say make it real? What is
the use and meaning of realizing? Or if you say the will is and
means realization, then do you not see that the will means the
identity of the pure and sensuous nature, that it implies the two
sides, and that "formal will" says, "have both sides, but be sure
you have only one"; or, more briefly, that pure or formal will is
nonsense?

In its simplest form the contradiction is this. "Realize noncontradiction" is the order. But "noncontradiction" = bare form;
"realize" = give content to; content contradicts form without
content; and so "realize noncontradiction" means "realize a contradiction."[6]

(2) In our remarks on the self-contradiction of the principle,
its abstract negation of reality on the one side and its demand

[6] The hopeless inconsistencies of the dualistic moral theory, the standing
contradictions of its moral theology and practical postulates generally, are

for realization on the other, we have perhaps rendered further detail needless; but it may be instructive to repeat more specially the general refutation.

We saw that an act of will has two sides, an inner and an outer, what (in one meaning of these much misused terms) we may call a "subjective" and an "objective" side. There is a certain content which on one side is to be done, on the other side is done. The killing of a man, for instance, is not, properly speaking, an act of my will unless I meant to kill him and did kill him. Neither the mere movement of my body, nor the mere thought of my mind, constitutes an act.[7]

There are two sides and on each side the content is the same. The doing *what* one wills is acting, and nothing else is acting. The act is the process of translation from the inside world to the outside world (or from the thought to the fact of an event in the inside world), and the translation would not be a translation unless it implied the identity of the translated.

The immediate corollary from this is that no act can be the mere carrying out of an abstract principle. The content on each side must be the same, and it is at once obvious that no abstraction is a content which is capable of real existence. To take its place in the outward world, the principle must be specialized into a concrete individual which can then be carried over into existence in time and space. Hence, on the inside (the "subjective" side), the abstraction must have become concrete and in itself have two sides, be in short individualized; or else there is no possibility of action, because nothing that can be carried over.[8]

beyond our subject. The whole point of view has been criticized in the second of the passages from Hegel referred to above.

We may remark in passing a contradiction involved in the doctrine of the imperative. A command is addressed by one will to another and must be obeyed, if at all, by the second will. But here the will that is commanded is not the will that executes; hence the imperative is never obeyed and, as it is not to produce action in that to which it is addressed, it is a mere sham-imperative.

[7] This statement is subject to the qualifications mentioned in Essay I, p. 7.

[8] Our statement must not be taken to deny the possibility of the will

Everybody knows that the only way to do your duty is to do your duties; that general doing good may mean doing no good in particular, and so none at all, but rather perhaps the contrary of good. Everybody knows that the setting out, whether in religion, morals, or politics, with the intent to realize an abstraction, is a futile endeavor; and that what it comes to is that either you do nothing at all, or that the particular content which is necessary for action is added to the abstraction by the chance of circumstances or caprice. Everybody suspects, if they do not feel sure, that the acting consciously on and from abstract principles means self-deceit or hypocrisy or both.

(3) A more psychological consideration leads us still to the futility of duty for duty's sake. A will which does not act is no will, and every act is a particular event; an act is this or that act, and an act in general is nonsense. But how can a formal act be this or that act? Even where the abstraction has been specialized into definite "material" ends and aims to be accomplished, yet even there for the particular volition the special circumstances of time, place, etc., are wanted. They may not be essential to the act; they may make no practical difference to the content. If I have resolved to kill a man in a certain way, the place, time, etc., are psychically necessary for the particular act of killing, but they may not enter into the essence of the act. (So it is with one's ordinary duties.) The more specialized and materialized the previous intent, the less is added to it by the particular circumstances; and the less specialized the content, the more is added. If I run out into the street to kill a man, chance[9] decides who it is I kill. So with duty. If I intend to do duty generally, chance decides what duty I do; for what falls outside the preconceived intent is chance, and here everything falls outside saving the bare form.

To act you must will something, and something definite. To will in general is impossible, and to will in particular is never to having a content which is *merely* this or that. We say nothing about that because we are not concerned with it.

[9] Chance, that is to say, relatively to my intent; because my intent does not essentially involve the particular person killed.

will nothing but a form. It must at best be to will a chance case
of the form, and then (speaking psychologically) what moves is
chance (desire). The bare form cannot move. Will, when one
wills nothing in particular, is a pure fiction; and (to put the same
thing differently) so is will without desire, conscious or unconscious, special or habitual. It is simply a psychological monster.
It is admitted that, if real, it is inexplicable; it is admitted to be
in no single case verifiable; and surely Schopenhauer (*op. cit.*
p. 168) is not wrong when he says that, if what is neither
conceivable nor to be found in experience is not incredible, then
nothing is incredible. If any theory requires such a supposition
then that proves the theory to be false.

We have shown that a formal will is self-contradictory since the
essence of will is that it should not be formal. Duty for duty's
sake is false and impossible. It may not be superfluous to show
in addition that even if such a principle of action were possible
yet it would be worthless and of no avail for practice.

The maxim of noncontradiction is useless. We have seen
that it contradicts itself, since it posits a content which is the contradiction of its bare form; but apart from that it gives us no
information. What am I to do? "Produce a tautology" is the
answer. "Everything which contradicts itself is wrong. Everything which is tautological is right. Nothing which is tautological
is wrong." Then what does contradict itself? Everything in one
sense; nothing in another.

The principle of noncontradiction does not mean Do not contradict your*self;* produce a harmony, a system in your acts and
yourself; realize yourself as an organic whole. That would be
vague enough without further directions, but what our principle
here says is not that. It says the *act* must not contradict itself.
What does this mean? It means that the matter realized, the
determination posited by the act, must be self-consistent. Property *e. g.* is self-consistent. Theft of property is a contradiction.

In the first place, however, is any determination free from contradiction? Take what you will, you must take something definite, and the definite is what it is by the negation of something

else. It belongs to the essence of any possible A that it should be not B, C, D, etc., and without this negation it would not be A. A mere positive affirmative is a fictitious abstraction. "Affirm A" means "negate B, C, D, etc." Property *e. g.* implies in its appropriation a negation, an exclusion. In this sense not only is the definite content in contradiction with the form, but it also in itself involves contradiction.

This, however, is not the meaning of the rule of noncontradiction. The meaning of that is that you must not posit a determination and with it its own negation. You must not have an act which embodies the rule to negate anything, for that is a self-contradiction. A rule "negate A" contradicts itself, for if A is negated you cannot negate it. "Steal property" is a contradiction, for it destroys property and with it possibility of theft.

We have no need here to push further a metaphysical argument against this view, for it supplies us at once with a crushing instance against itself. The essence of morality was a similar contradiction.[10] "Negate the sensuous self." But if the sensuous self *is* negated, possibility of morality disappears. Morality is thus as inconsistent as theft. "Succor the poor" both negates *and* presupposes (hence posits) poverty: as Blake comically says,

> Pity would be no more,
> If we did not make somebody poor.

If you are to love your enemies you must never be without them; and yet you try to get rid of them. Is that consistent? In short, every duty which presupposes something to be negated is no duty; it is an immoral rule because self-contradictory.

No rule must be stated negatively then, but all positively; and then comes the very serious question whether there is any rule which can *not* be stated positively. The canon is an empty form, "Let A be A." It is a tautology; and it requires no great skill to put anything and everything into the form of a tautology, and so to moralize it. "Let property be," "let no property be"; "let

---

[10] Hegel (*loc. cit.*) pushes this ruthlessly even against the postulate of immortality. In what immediately follows we are drawing from him very largely.

law be," "let no law be"; "let love be," "let hate be"; "be brave," "be cowardly"; "be kind," "be cruel," "be indifferent"; "let succor be," "let no succor be"; or riches, or poverty, or pleasure, or pain. Where is the canon? It is nowhere. Poverty is poverty and is an affirmative tautology. Hate is hate, as much as love is love. They become contradictory only when you say, "hate your friends," or "love your enemies"; or when, instead of affirming, you analyze them and see that each is the affirmation of a negation, or the negation of an affirmation. Hate we can all see is so, and deeper thinkers tell us the same of love.

What duty for duty's sake really does is first to posit a determination, such as property, love, courage, etc., and then to say that whatever contradicts these is wrong. And since the principle is a formal empty universal, there is no connection between it and the content which is brought under it. That connection is made from the outside and rests on arbitrary choice, or considerations of general well-being and perhaps pleasure. The morality of pure duty turns out then to be either something like a Hedonistic rule,[11] or no rule at all save the hypocritical maxim that before you do what you like you should call it duty, and this outdoes Probabilism.

Thus to get from the form of duty to particular duties is impossible. The particular duties must be taken for granted, as in ordinary morality they are taken for granted. But supposing this done, is duty for duty's sake a valid formula in the sense that we are to act always on a law and nothing but a law, and that a law can have no exceptions, in the sense of particular cases where it is overruled? No, this takes for granted that life is so simple that we never have to consider more than one duty at a time; whereas we really have to do with conflicting duties, which as a rule escape conflict simply because it is understood which have to give way. It is a mistake to suppose that collision of duties is uncommon; it has been remarked truly that *every* act can be taken to involve such collision.

To put the question plainly—It is clear that in a given case I may have several duties, and that I may be able to do only one.

[11] Schopenhauer has some characteristic and piquant criticism on this head.

I must then break some "categorical" law, and the question the
ordinary man puts to himself is, Which duty am I to do? He
would say, "all duties have their limits and are subordinated one
to another. You cannot put them all in the form of your 'categorical imperative' (in the shape of a law absolute and dependent
on nothing beside itself) without such exceptions and modifica-
tions that, in many cases, you might as well have left it alone
altogether. We certainly have laws but we may not be able to
follow them all at once, and to know which we are to follow is
a matter of good sense which cannot be decided any other way.
One should give to the poor—in what cases and how much?
Should sacrifice oneself—in what way and within what limits?
Should not indulge one's appetites—except when it is right. Should
not idle away one's time—except when one takes one's pleasure.
Nor neglect one's work—but for some good reason. All these
points we admit are in one way matter of law; but if you think
to decide in particular cases by applying some 'categorical
imperative,' you must be a pedant, if not a fool."

Ordinary morality does not hold to each of its laws as inviolable,
each as an absolute end in itself. It is not even aware of a collision in most cases where duties clash; and, where it perceives it,
and is confronted with collisions of moral laws, each of which
it has been accustomed to look on as an absolute monarch, so to
speak, or a commander-in-chief, rather than a possible subordinate
officer, there it does subordinate one to the other, and feels
uneasiness only in proportion to the rarity of the necessity, and
the consequent jar to the feelings. There are few laws a breach
of which (in obedience to a higher law) morality does not allow,
and I believe there are none which are not to be broken in
conceivable (imaginable) circumstances, though the necessity of
deciding the question does not practically occur. According to
ordinary morality (the fact is too palpable to be gainsaid), it is
quite right to speak falsely with intent to deceive under certain
circumstances, though ordinary morality might add, "I don't call
that a lie." It *is* a lie; and when Kant and others maintained that
it must always be wrong to lie, they forgot the rather important
fact that in some cases to abstain from acting *is* acting, is wilful

neglect of a duty, and that there are duties above truth-speaking, and many offenses against morality which are worse, though they may be less painful, than a lie. So to kill oneself in a manner which must be called suicide *may* not only be right but heroic;[12] homicide may be excusable, rebellion in the subject and disobedience in the soldier all morally justifiable, and every one of them clear breaches of categorical imperatives, in obedience to a higher law.

All that it comes to is this (and it is, we must remember, a very important truth), that you must never break a law of duty to please yourself, never for the sake of an end not duty, but only for the sake of a superior and overruling duty. Any breach of duty, as duty and not as *lower* duty, is always and absolutely wrong; but it would be rash to say that any one act must be in all cases absolutely and unconditionally immoral. Circumstances decide because circumstances determine the manner in which the overruling duty must be realized. This is a simple fact which by the candid observer cannot be denied, and which is merely the exposition of the moral consciousness, though I am fully aware that it is an exposition which that consciousness would not accept, simply because it must necessarily misunderstand it in its abstract form. And if moral theory were meant to influence moral practice and to be dabbled in by "the vulgar" (and there are not so many persons who in this respect are *not* the vulgar), then I grant this is a fact it would be well to keep in the background. None the less it is a fact.[13]

So we see "duty for duty's sake" says only, "do the right for the

[12] The story of the imprisoned Italian who, knowing that he was being drugged to disorder his intellect and cause him to betray his comrades, opened a vein, is a good instance. It is a duty for various persons continually to give themselves to certain or well-nigh certain death, and no one has ever called it anything but heroically right and dutiful. Excusable killing is illustrated by the well-known story told in the Indian Mutiny of the husband who killed his wife. Rebellions and mutinies need no illustration. It is noticeable that Berkeley urged passive obedience on the ground that a moral law was absolute.

[13] We shall come upon this again in Essays V and VI.

sake of the right"; it does not tell us what right is; or "realize a good will, do what a good will would do, for the sake of being yourself a good will." And that is something, but beyond that it is silent or beside the mark. It tells us to act for the sake of a form, which we saw was a self-contradictory command; and we even saw that in sober sadness the form did exist for form's sake, and in literal truth remained only a form. We saw that duty's universal laws are not universal if that means they can never be overruled, and that its form and its absolute imperative are impracticable. What after all remains is the acting for the sake of a good will, to realize oneself by realizing the will which is above us and higher than ours; and the assurance that this, and not the self to be pleased, is the end for which we have to live. But as to that which the good will is, it tells us nothing, and leaves us with an idle abstraction.

MY STATION AND ITS DUTIES

W E have traversed by this time, however cursorily, a considerable field, and so far it might appear without any issue or at best with a merely negative result. Certainly in our anticipatory remarks (Essay II), we thought we found some answer to the question, What is the end? But that answer was too abstract to stand by itself. And, if we may be said to know thus much, that the end is self-realization, yet at present we do not seem to have learned anything about the self to be realized. And the detail of Essays II and III appears at most to have given us some knowledge of that which self-realization is not.

We have learned that the self to be realized is not the self as this or that feeling, or as any series of the particular feelings of our own or others' streams or trains of consciousness. It is, in short, not the self to be pleased. The greatest sum of units of pleasure we found to be the idea of a mere collection, whereas, if we wanted morality, it was something like a universal that we wanted. Happiness, as the effort to construct that universal by the addition of particulars, gave us a futile and bastard product which carried its self-destruction within it, in the continual assertion of its own universality, together with its unceasing actual particularity and finitude; so that happiness was, if we chose, nowhere not realized; or again, if we chose, not anywhere realizable. And passing then to the opposite pole, to the universal as the negative of the particulars, to the supposed pure will or duty for duty's sake, we found that too was an unreal conception. It was a mere form which, to be will, must give itself a content, and which could give itself a content only at the cost of a self-contradiction. We saw, further, that any such content was in addition arbitrarily postulated and that, even then, the form was either never realized, because real in no particular content, or always and everywhere realized, because equally reconcilable with any content. And so, as before with happiness, we perceived that morality could have no existence if it meant anything more than the continual assevera-

tion of an empty formula. And, if we had chosen, we might
have gone on to exhibit the falsity of asceticism, to see that the
self cannot be realized as its own mere negation, since morality
is practice, is will to do something, is self-affirmation; and that a
will to deny one's will is not self-realization, but rather is, strictly
speaking, a psychical impossibility, a self-contradictory illusion.
And the possibility, again, of taking as the self to be realized the
self which I happen to have, my natural being, and of making
life the end of life in the sense that each should live his life as he
happens to find it in his own nature, has been precluded beforehand by the result derived from the consideration of the moral
consciousness, viz., that morality implies a superior, a higher self,
or at all events a universal something which is above this or that
self and so above mine. And, to complete the account of our
negations, we saw further, with respect to duty for duty's sake, that
even were it possible (as it is not) to create a content from the
formula and to elaborate in this manner a system of duties, yet
even then the practice required by the theory would be impossible,
and so too morality, since in practice particular duties must collide
and the collision of duties, if we hold to duty for duty's sake, is the
destruction of all duty save the unrealized form of duty in general.

But let us view this result, which seems so unsatisfactory, from
the positive side; let us see after all with what we are left. We
have self-realization left as the end, the self so far being defined as
neither a collection of particular feelings nor an abstract universal.
The self is to be realized as something not simply one or the other;
it is to be realized further as will, will not being merely the natural
will, or the will as it happens to exist and finds itself here or there,
but the will as the *good* will, *i. e.*, the will that realizes an end
which is above this or that man, superior to them, and capable of
confronting them in the shape of a law or an ought. This
superior something further, which is a possible law or ought to the
individual man, does not depend for its existence on his choice or
opinion. Either there is no morality, so says the moral consciousness, or moral duties exist independently of their position by this
or that person—my duty may be mine and no other man's, but I
do not make it mine. If it is duty, it would be the duty of any

person in my case and condition, whether they thought so or not—in a word, duty is "objective," in the sense of not being contingent on the opinion or choice of this or that subject.

What we have left then (to resume it) is this—the end is the realization of the good will which is superior to ourselves; and again the end is self-realization. Bringing these together we see the end is the realization of ourselves as the will which is above ourselves. And this will (if morality exists) we saw must be "objective," because not dependent on "subjective" liking; and "universal," because not identifiable with any particular, but standing above all actual and possible particulars. Further, though universal it is not abstract since it belongs to its essence that it should be realized, and it has no real existence except in and through its particulars. The good will (for morality) is meaningless, if, whatever else it be, it be not the will of living human beings. It is a concrete universal because it not only is above but is within and throughout its details, and is so far only as they are. It is the life which can live only in and by them, as they are dead unless within it; it is the whole soul which lives so far as the body lives, which makes the body a living body and which without the body is as unreal an abstraction as the body without it. It is an organism and a moral organism; and it is conscious self-realization because only by the will of its self-conscious members can the moral organism give itself reality. It is the self-realization of the whole body because it is one and the same will which lives and acts in the life and action of each. It is the self-realization of each member because each member cannot find the function which makes him himself, apart from the whole to which he belongs; to be himself he must go beyond himself, to live his life he must live a life which is not *merely* his own, but which, none the less, but on the contrary all the more, is intensely and emphatically his own individuality. Here, and here first, are the contradictions which have beset us solved—here is a universal which can confront our wandering desires with a fixed and stern imperative, but which yet is no unreal form of the mind but a living soul that penetrates and stands fast in the detail of actual existence. It is real, and real for me. It is in its affirmation that

I affirm myself, for I am but as a "heart-beat in its system." And I am real in it, for, when I give myself to it, it gives me the fruition of my own personal activity, the accomplished ideal of my life which is happiness. In the realized idea which, superior to me and yet here and now in and by me, affirms itself in a continuous process, we have found the end, we have found self-realization, duty, and happiness in one—yes, we have found ourselves when we have found our station and its duties, our function as an organ in the social organism.

"Mere rhetoric," we shall be told, "a bad metaphysical dream, a stale old story once more warmed up, which cannot hold its own against the logic of facts. That the state was prior to the individual, that the whole was sometimes more than the sum of the parts, was an illusion which preyed on the thinkers of Greece. But that illusion has been traced to its source and dispelled and is in plain words exploded. The family, society, the state, and generally every community of men consists of individuals, and there is nothing in them real except the individuals. Individuals have made them, and make them, by placing themselves and by standing in certain relations. The individuals are real by themselves and it is because of them that the relations are real. They make them, they are real *in* them, not because of them, and they would be just as real *out* of them. The whole is the mere sum of the parts, and the parts are as real away from the whole as they are within the whole. Do you really suppose that the individual would perish if every form of community were destroyed? Do you think that anything real answers to the phrases of universal and organism? Everything is in the organism what it is out, and the universal is a name, the existing fact answering to which is particular persons in such and such relations. To put the matter shortly, the community is the sum of its parts, is made by the addition of parts, and the parts are as real before the addition as after; the relations they stand in do not make them what they are, but are accidental, not essential, to their being; and, as to the whole, if it is not a name for the individuals that compose it, it is a name of nothing actual. These are not metaphysical dreams. They are facts and verifiable facts."

Are they facts? Facts should explain facts; and the view called "individualism" (because the one reality that it believes in is the "individual," in the sense of this, that, and the other particular) should hence be the right explanation. What are the facts here to be explained? They are human communities, the family, society, and the state. Individualism has explained them long ago. They are "collections" held together by force, illusion, or contract. It has told the story of their origin and to its own satisfaction cleared the matter up. Is the explanation satisfactory and verifiable? That would be a bold assertion when historical science has rejected and entirely discredited the individualistic origin of society, and when, if we turn to practice, we find everywhere the state asserting itself as a power which has, and, if need be, asserts the right to make use of and expend the property and person of the individual without regard to his wishes, and which, moreover, may destroy his life in punishment, and put forth other powers such as no theory of contract will explain except by the most palpable fictions, while at the same time no ordinary person calls their morality in question. Both history and practical politics refuse to verify the "facts" of the individualist; and we should find still less to confirm his theory if we examined the family.

If, then, apart from metaphysic one looks at the history and present practice of society, these would not appear to establish the "fact" that the individual is the one reality and communities mere collections. "For all that," we shall be told, "it is the truth." True that is, I suppose, not as fact but as metaphysic; and this is what one finds too often with those who deride metaphysic and talk most of facts. Their minds, so far as such a thing may be, are not seldom mere "collective unities" of metaphysical dogmas. They decry any real metaphysic because they dimly feel that their own will not stand criticism; and they appeal to facts because while their metaphysic stands they feel they need not be afraid of them. When their view is pushed as to plain realities, such as the nature of gregarious animals, the probable origin of mankind from them, the institutions of early society, actual existing communities with the common type impressed on all their members, their organic structure and the assertion of the whole body as of paramount importance in comparison with any of the members, then they must fall back on their metaphysic. And the point we wish here to emphasize is this, that their metaphysic is mere dogmatism. It is assumed, not proved. It has a right to no refutation, for assertion can demand no more than counter-assertion; and what is affirmed on the one side we on the other side can simply deny, and we intend to do so here.

A discussion that would go to the bottom of the question, What is an individual? is certainly wanted. It would certainly be desirable, showing first what an individual is, to show then that "individualism" has not apprehended that, but taken an abstraction for reality. But, if I could do that (which I could not do), this would not be the place; nor perhaps should I have to say very much that has not been said before, and has not been attended to.

But we are not going to enter on a metaphysical question to which we are not equal; we meet the metaphysical assertion of the "individualist" with a mere denial and, turning to facts, we will try to show that they lead us in another direction. To the assertion, then, that selves are "individual" in the sense of exclusive of other selves, we oppose the (equally justified) assertion that this is a mere fancy. We say that, out of theory, no such individual men exist; and we will try to show from fact that, in fact, what we call an individual man is what he is because of and by virtue of community, and that communities are thus not mere names but something real, and can be regarded (if we mean to keep to facts) only as the one in the many.

And to confine the subject and to keep to what is familiar, we will not call to our aid the life of animals, nor early societies, nor the course of history, but we will take men as they are now; we will take ourselves and endeavor to keep wholly to the teaching of experience.

Let us take a man, an Englishman as he is now, and try to point out that apart from what he has in common with others, apart from his sameness with others, he is not an Englishman— nor a man at all; that if you take him as something by himself, he is not what he is. Of course we do not mean to say that he cannot go out of England without disappearing, nor, even if all the rest of the nation perished that he would not survive. What we mean to say is that he is what he is because he is a born and educated social being, and a member of an individual social organism; that if you make abstraction of all this, which is the same in him and in others, what you have left is not an Englishman, nor a man, but some I know not what residuum, which never has existed by itself and does not so exist. If we suppose the world of relations, in which he was born and bred, never to have been, then we suppose the very essence of him not to be; if we take that away, we have taken him away; and hence he now is not an individual, in the sense of owing nothing to the sphere of relations in which he finds himself, but does contain those relations within himself as belonging to his very being; he is what he is, in brief, so far as he is what others also are.

But we shall be cut short here with an objection. "It is impossible," we shall be told, "that two men should have the *same* thing in common. You are confusing sameness and likeness." I say in answer that I am not, and that the too probable objector I am imagining too probably knows the meaning of neither one word nor the other. But this is a matter we do not intend to stay over, because it is a metaphysical question we cannot discuss, and which, moreover, we cannot be called on to discuss. We cannot be called on to discuss it because we have to do again here with sheer assertion, which either is ignorant of or ignores the critical investigation of the subject, and which, therefore, has no right to demand an answer. We allude to it merely because it has become a sort of catchword with "advanced thinkers." All that it comes to is this: first identity and diversity are assumed to exclude one another, and therefore, since diversity is a fact, it follows that there is no identity. Hence a difficulty; because it has been seen long ago and forces itself upon everyone, that denial of all identity brings you into sharp collision with ordinary fact and leads to total skepticism[1]; so, to avoid this,

[1] Even from Mr. Mill (in controversy) we can quote, "If every general conception, instead of being 'the One in the Many,' were considered to be as many different conceptions as there are things to which it is applicable, there would be no such thing as general language."—*Logic*, 6th ed., I, 201.

while we yet maintain the previous dogma, "resemblance" is brought in—a conception which (I suppose I need not add) is not analyzed or properly defined, and so does all the better. Against these assertions I shall put some others, viz., that identity and diversity, sameness and difference, imply one another, and depend for their meaning on one another; that mere diversity is nonsense, just as mere identity is also nonsense; that resemblance or likeness, strictly speaking, falls not in the objects, but in the person contemplating (likening, *ver-gleichend*) ; that "is A really like B?" does not mean "does it seem like?" It may mean "would it seem like to everybody?" but it generally means "is there an 'objective identity'? Is there a point or points the same in both, whether anyone sees it or not?" We do not talk of cases of "mistaken likeness"; we do not hang one man because he is "exactly like" another, or at least we do not wish to do so. We are the same as we were, not merely more or less like. We have the same faith, hope, and purpose, and the same feelings as another man has now, as ourselves had at another time—not understanding thereby the numerical indistinguishedness of particular states and moments, but calling the feelings one and the same feeling because *what* is felt is the same, and not merely like. In short, so far is it from being true that "sameness" is really "likeness," that it is utterly false that two things are really and objectively "like," unless that means "more or less the same." So much by way of counter-assertion; and now let us turn to our facts.

The "individual" man, the man into whose essence his community with others does not enter, who does not include relation to others in his very being, is, we say, a fiction, and in the light of facts we have to examine him. Let us take him in the shape of an English child as soon as he is born; for I suppose we ought not to go further back. Let us take him as soon as he is separated from his mother and occupies a space clear and exclusive of all other human beings. At this time, education and custom will, I imagine, be allowed to have not as yet operated on him or lessened his "individuality." But is he now a mere "individual," in the sense of not implying in his being identity with others? We cannot say that if we hold to the teaching of modern physiology.

Physiology would tell us, in one language or another, that even now the child's mind is no passive "tabula rasa"; he has an inner, a yet undeveloped nature, which must largely determine his future individuality. What is this inner nature? Is it particular to himself? Certainly not all of it, will have to be the answer. The child is not fallen from heaven. He is born of certain parents who come of certain families, and he has in him the qualities of his parents, and, as breeders would say, of the strains from both sides. Much of it we can see and more we believe to be latent and, given certain (possible or impossible) conditions, ready to come to light. On the descent of mental qualities modern investigation and popular experience, as expressed in uneducated vulgar opinion, altogether, I believe, support one another, and we need not linger here. But if the intellectual and active qualities do descend from ancestors, is it not, I would ask, quite clear that a man may have in him the same that his father and mother had, the same that his brothers and sisters have? And if anyone objects to the word "same," I would put this to him. If, concerning two dogs allied in blood, I were to ask a man, "Is that of the same strain or stock as this?" and were answered, "No, not the same, but similar," should I not think one of these things, that the man either meant to deceive me, or was a "thinker," or a fool?

But the child is not merely the member of a family; he is born into other spheres, and (passing over the subordinate wholes which nevertheless do in many cases qualify him) he is born a member of the English nation. It is, I believe, a matter of fact that at birth the child of one race is not the same as the child of another; that in the children of the one race there is a certain identity, a developed or undeveloped national type which may be hard to recognize, or which at present may even be unrecognizable, but which nevertheless in some form will appear. If that be the fact, then again we must say that one English child is in some points, though perhaps it does not as yet show itself, the same as another. His being is so far common to him with others; he is not a mere "individual."

We see the child has been born at a certain time of parents of a certain race, and that means also of a certain degree of culture.

It is the opinion of those best qualified to speak on the subject that civilization is to some not inconsiderable extent hereditary; that aptitudes are developed, and are latent in the child at birth; and that it is a very different thing, even apart from education, to be born of civilized and of uncivilized ancestors. These "civilized tendencies," if we may use the phrase, are part of the essence of the child. He would only partly (if at all) be himself without them; he owes them to his ancestors, and his ancestors owe them to society. The ancestors were made what they were by the society they lived in. If in answer it be replied, "Yes, but individual ancestors were prior to their society," then that, to say the least of it, is a hazardous and unproved assertion, since man, so far as history can trace him back, is social; and if Mr. Darwin's conjecture as to the development of man from a social animal be received, we must say that man has never been anything but social, and society never was made by individual men. Nor, if the (baseless) assertion of the priority of individual men were allowed, would that destroy our case, for certainly our more immediate ancestors were social; and, whether society was manufactured previously by individuals or not, yet in their case it certainly was not so. They at all events have been so qualified by the common possessions of social mankind that, as members in the organism, they have become relative to the whole. If we suppose then that the results of the social life of the race are present in a latent and potential form in the child, can we deny that they are common property? Can we assert that they are not an element of sameness in all? Can we say that the individual is this individual because he is exclusive, when, if we deduct from him what he includes, he loses characteristics which make him himself, and when again he does include what the others include, and therefore does (how can we escape the consequence?) include in some sense the others also, just as they include him? By himself, then, what are we to call him? I confess I do not know unless we name him a theoretical attempt to isolate what cannot be isolated, and that, I suppose, has, out of our heads, no existence. But what he is really, and not in mere theory, can be described only as the specification or particularization of that which is common, which is the same amid diversity, and without which the "individual" would be so other than he is that we could not call him the same.

Thus the child is at birth; and he is born not into a desert, but into a living world, a whole which has a true individuality of its own, and into a system and order which it is difficult to look at as anything else than an organism, and which, even in England, we are now beginning to call by that name. And I fear that the "individuality" (the particularness) which the child brought into the light with him now stands but a poor chance, and that there is no help for him until he is old enough to become a "philosopher." We have seen that already he has in him inherited habits, or what will of themselves appear as such; but, in addition to this, he is not for one moment left alone, but continually tampered with; and the habituation which is applied from the outside is the more insidious that it answers to this inborn disposition. Who can resist it? Nay, who but a "thinker" could wish to have resisted it? And yet the tender care that receives and guides him is impressing on him habits, habits, alas, not particular to himself, and the "icy chains" of universal custom are hardening themselves round his cradled life. As the poet tells us, he has not yet thought of himself; his earliest notions come mixed to him of things and persons, not distinct from one another, nor divided from the feeling of his own existence. The need that he cannot understand moves him to foolish, but not futile, cries for what only another can give him; and the breast of his mother, and the soft warmth and touches and tones of his nurse, are made one with the feeling of his own pleasure and pain; nor is he yet a moralist to beware of such illusion and to see in them mere means to an end without them in his separate self. For he does not even think of his separate self; he grows with his world, his mind fills and orders itself; and when he can separate himself from that world, and know himself apart from it, then by that time his self, the object of his self-consciousness, is penetrated, infected, characterized by the existence of others. Its content implies in every fiber relations of community. He learns, or already perhaps has learned, to speak, and here he appropriates the common heritage of his race; the tongue that he makes his own is his country's language, it is (or it should be) the same that others speak, and it carries into his mind the ideas and sentiments of the race (over this I need not stay), and stamps them in indelibly. He grows up in an atmosphere of example and general custom, his life widens out from one little world to other and higher worlds, and he apprehends through successive stations the whole in which he lives, and in which he has lived. Is he now to try and develop his "individuality," his self which is not the same as other selves? Where is it? What is it? Where can he find it? The soul within him is saturated, is filled, is qualified by, it has assimilated, has got its substance, has built itself up from, it *is* one and the same life with the universal life, and if he turns against this he turns against himself; if he thrusts it from him, he tears his own vitals; if he attacks it, he sets his weapon against his own heart. He has found his life in the life of the whole, he lives that in himself, "he is a pulse-beat of the whole system, and himself the whole system."

"The child, in his character of the form of the possibility of a moral individual, is something subjective or negative; his growing to manhood is the ceasing to be of this form, and his education is the discipline or the compulsion thereof. The positive side and the essence is that he is suckled at the breast of the universal Ethos, lives in its absolute intuition, as in that of a foreign being first, then comprehends it more and more, and so passes over into the universal mind." The writer proceeds to draw the weighty conclusion that virtue "is not a troubling oneself about a peculiar and isolated morality of one's own, that the striving for a positive morality of one's own is futile, and in its very nature impossible of attainment; that in respect of morality the saying of the wisest men of antiquity is the only one which is true, that to be moral is to live in accordance with the moral tradition of one's country; and in respect of education the one true answer is that which a Pythagorean gave to him who asked what was the best education for his son, If you make him the citizen of a people with good institutions."[2]

[2] Hegel, *Philosophische Abhandlungen*, I, 389.

But this is to anticipate. So far, I think, without aid from metaphysics, we have seen that the "individual" apart from the community is an abstraction. It is not anything real and hence not anything that we can realize, however much we may wish to do so. We have seen that I am myself by sharing with others, by including in my essence relations to them, the relations of the social state. If I wish to realize my true being I must therefore realize something beyond my being as a mere this or that, for my true being has in it a life which is not the life of any mere particular, and so must be called a universal life.

What is it then that I am to realize? We have said it in "my station and its duties." To know what a man is (as we have seen) you must not take him in isolation. He is one of a people, he was born in a family, he lives in a certain society, in a certain state. What he has to do depends on what his place is, what his function is, and that all comes from his station in the organism. Are there then such organisms in which he lives, and if so, what is their nature? Here we come to questions which must be answered in full by any complete system of Ethics, but which we cannot enter on. We must content ourselves by pointing out that there are such facts as the family, then in a middle position a man's own profession and society, and, over all, the larger community of the state. Leaving out of sight the question of a society wider than the state, we must say that a man's life with its moral duties is in the main filled up by his station in that system of wholes which the state is, and that this, partly by its laws and institutions and still more by its spirit, gives him the life which he does live and ought to live. That objective institutions exist is of course an obvious fact; and it is a fact which every day is becoming plainer that these institutions are organic, and further, that they are moral. The assertion that communities have been manufactured by the addition of exclusive units is, as we have seen, a mere fable; and if, within the state, we take that which seems wholly to depend on individual caprice, e. g., marriage,[3]

[3] Marriage is a contract, a contract to pass out of the sphere of contract; and this is possible only because the contracting parties are already beyond and above the sphere of mere contract.

yet even here we find that a man does give up his self so far as it excludes others; he does bring himself under a unity which is superior to the particular person and the impulses that belong to his single existence, and which makes him fully as much as he makes it. In short, man is a social being; he is real only because he is social, and can realize himself only because it is as social that he realizes himself. The mere individual is a delusion of theory; and the attempt to realize it in practice is the starvation and mutilation of human nature, with total sterility or the production of monstrosities.

Let us now in detail compare the advantages of our present view with the defects of "duty for duty's sake." The objections we found fatal to that view may be stated as follows: (1) The universal was abstract. There was no content which belonged to it and was one with it; and the consequence was that either nothing could be willed, or what was willed was willed not because of the universal, but capriciously. (2) The universal was "subjective." It certainly gave itself out as "objective," in the sense of being independent of this or that person, but still it was not real in the world. It did not come to us as what *was*, it came as what (merely) was to be, an inner notion in moral persons, which had not power to carry itself out and transform the world. And self-realization, if it means will, does mean that we put ourselves forth and see ourselves actual in outer existence. Hence, by identifying ourselves with that which has not this existence, which is not master of the outer world, we cannot secure our self-realization; since, when we have identified ourselves with the end, the end may still remain a mere inner end which does not accomplish itself, and so does not satisfy us. (3) The universal left a part of ourselves outside it. However much we tried to be good, however determined we were to make our will one with the good will, yet we never succeeded. There was always something left in us which was in contradiction with the good. And this we saw was even necessary because morality meant and implied this contradiction, unless we accepted that form of conscientiousness which consists in the simple identification of one's conscience with one's own self (unless, *i. e.*, the consciousness of the relation of my private self to myself as the good self be degraded into my self-consciousness of my mere private self as the good self); and this cannot be if we are in earnest with morality. There thus remains a perpetual contradiction in myself, no less than in the world, between the "is to be" and the "is," a contradiction that cannot be got rid of without getting rid of morality; for, as we saw, it is inherent in morality. The man cannot realize himself in himself as moral because the conforming of his sensuous nature to the universal would be the entire suppression of it, and hence not only of himself but also of the morality which is constituted by the relation of himself to the universal law. The man then cannot find self-realization in the morality of pure duty because (1) he cannot look on his subjective self as the realized moral law; (2) he cannot look on the objective world as the realization of the moral law; (3) he cannot realize the moral law at all because it is defined as that which has no particular content, and therefore no reality; or, if he gives it a content, then it is not the law he realizes, since the content is got not from the law but from elsewhere. In short, duty for duty's sake is an unsolved contradiction, the standing "is to be," which, therefore, because it is to be, is *not;* and in which, therefore, since it is *not,* he cannot find himself realized nor satisfy himself.

These are serious defects. Let us see how they are mended by "my station and its duties." In that (1) the universal is concrete, (2) it is objective, (3) it leaves nothing of us outside it.

(1) It is concrete, and yet not given by caprice. Let us take the latter first. It is not given by caprice for, although within certain limits I may choose my station according to my own liking, yet I and everyone else must have some station with duties pertaining to it, and those duties do not depend on our opinion or liking. Certain circumstances, a certain position, call for a certain course. How I in particular know what my right course is, is a question we shall recur to hereafter—but at present we may take it as an obvious fact that in my station my particular duties are prescribed to me, and I have them whether I wish to or not. And secondly, it is concrete. The universal to be realized is no abstraction, but an organic whole; a system where many spheres

are subordinated to one sphere, and particular actions to spheres. This system is real in the detail of its functions, not out of them, and lives in its vital processes, not away from them. The organs are always at work for the whole, the whole is at work in the organs. And I am one of the organs. The universal then which I am to realize is the system which penetrates and subordinates to itself the particulars of all lives, and here and now in my life has this and that function in this and that case, in exercising which through my will it realizes itself as a whole, and me in it.

(2) It is "objective"; and this means that it does not stand over against the outer world as mere "subject" confronted by mere "object." In that sense of the words it is neither merely "objective" nor merely "subjective"; but it is that real identity of subject and object, which, as we have seen, is the only thing that satisfies our desires. The inner side does exist, but it is no more than the inside; it is one factor in the whole and must not be separated from the other factor; and the mistake which is made by the morality which confines itself to the individual man is just this attempt at the separation of what cannot be separated. The inner side certainly is a fact, and it can be distinguished from the rest of the whole; but it really is one element of the whole, depends on the whole for its being, and cannot be divided from it. Let us explain. The moral world, as we said, is a whole, and has two sides. There is an outer side, systems and institutions, from the family to the nation; this we may call the body of the moral world. And there must also be a soul, or else the body goes to pieces; everyone knows that institutions without the spirit of them are dead. In the moral organism this spirit is in the will of the organs as the will of the whole which, in and by the organs, carries out the organism and makes it alive, and which also (and this is the point to which attention is requested) is and must be felt or known in each organ as his own inward and personal will. It is quite clear that a nation is not strong without public spirit, and is not public spirited unless the members of it are public spirited, *i. e.*, feel the good of the public as a personal matter, or have it at their hearts. The point here is that you cannot have the moral world unless it is willed; that to be willed it must be

willed by persons; and that these persons not only have the moral world as the content of their wills, but also must in some way be aware of themselves as willing this content. This being inwardly aware of oneself as willing the good will falls in the inside of the moral whole; we may call it the soul; and it is the sphere of personal morality, or morality in the narrower sense of the consciousness of the relation of my private self to the inwardly presented universal will, my being aware of and willing myself as one with that or contrary to that, as dutiful or bad. We must never let this out of our sight, that, where the moral world exists, you have and you must have these two sides; neither will stand apart from the other; moral institutions are carcasses without personal morality, and personal morality apart from moral institutions is an unreality, a soul without a body.

Now this inward, this "subjective," this personal side, this knowing in himself by the subject of the relation in which the will of him as this or that man stands to the will of the whole within him, or (as was rightly seen by "duty for duty's sake") this consciousness in the one subject of himself as two selves, is, as we said, necessary for all morality. But the form in which it is present may vary very much, and, beginning with the stage of mere feeling, goes on to that of explicit reflection. The reader who considers the matter will perceive that (whether in the life of mankind or of this or that man) we do not begin with a consciousness of good and evil, right and wrong, as such, or in the strict sense.[4] The child is taught to will a content which is universal and good, and he learns to identify his will with it so that he feels pleasure when he feels himself in accord with it, uneasiness or pain when his will is contrary thereto and he feels that it is contrary. This is the beginning of personal morality, and from this we may pass to consider the end. That, so far as form went, was sufficiently exhibited in Essay IV. It consists in the explicit consciousness in myself of two elements which, even though they exist in disunion, are felt to be really one; these are myself as the will of this or that self, and again the universal will as the will for good; and this latter I feel to be my true self, and desire my other self to be subordinated

[4] On this point see more in Essay VII.

to and so identified with it; in which case I feel the satisfaction
of an inward realization. That so far as form goes is correct.
But the important point on which "duty for duty's sake" utterly
failed us was as to the content of the universal will. We have
seen that for action this must have a content, and now we see
where the content comes from. The universal side in personal
morality is, in short, the reflection of the objective moral world
into ourselves (or into itself). The outer universal which I have
been taught to will as my will, and which I have grown to find
myself in, is now presented by me inwardly to myself as the universal which is my true being, and which by my will I must realize,
if need be, against my will as this or that man. So this inner universal has the same content as the outer universal, for it *is* the
outer universal in another sphere; it is the inside *of* the outside.
There was the whole system as an objective will, including my
station, and realizing itself here and now in my function. *Here* is
the same system presented as a will in me, standing above my will,
which wills a certain act to be done by me as a will which is one
with the universal will. This universal will is not a blank, but is
filled by the consideration of my station in the whole with reference to habitual and special acts. The ideal self appealed to by
the moral man is an ideally presented will, in his position and
circumstances, which rightly particularizes the general laws which
answer to the general functions and system of spheres of the moral
organism. That is the content, and therefore, as we saw, it is
concrete and filled. And therefore also (which is equally important) it is not merely "subjective."

If, on the inner side of the moral whole, the universal factor
were (as in would-be morality it is) filled with a content which is
not the detail of the objective will particularizing itself in such and
such functions, then there would be no true identity of subject
and object, no need why that which is moral should be that which
is real, and we should never escape from a practical postulate,
which, as we saw, is a practical standing contradiction. But if, as
we have seen, the universal on the inside is the universal on the
outside reflected in us, or (since we cannot separate it and ourselves) into itself in us; if the objective will of the moral organism

is real only in the will of its organs, and if, in willing morally, we will ourselves as that will, and that will wills itself in us—then we must hold that this universal on the inner side is the will of the whole, which is self-conscious in us, and wills itself in us against the actual or possible opposition of the false private self. This being so, when we will morally, the will of the objective world wills itself in us, and carries both us and itself out into the world of the moral will, which is its own realm. We see thus that when morals are looked at as a whole, the will of the inside, so far as it is moral, *is* the will of the outside, and the two are one and cannot be torn apart without *ipso facto* destroying the unity in which morality consists. To be moral I must will my station and its duties; that is, I will to particularize the moral system truly in a given case; and the other side to this act is that the moral system wills to particularize itself in a given station and functions, *i. e.*, in my actions and by my will. In other words, my moral self is not simply mine; it is not an inner which belongs simply to me; and further, it is not a mere inner at all, but it is the soul which animates the body and lives in it, and would not be the soul if it had not a body and *its* body. The objective organism, the systematized moral world, is the reality of the moral will; my duties on the inside answer to due functions on the outside. There is no need here for a pre-established or a postulated harmony, for the moral whole is the identity of both sides; my private choice, so far as I am moral, is the mere form of bestowing myself on and identifying myself with the will of the moral organism, which realizes in its process both itself and myself. Hence we see that what I have to do I have not to force on a recalcitrant world; I have to fill my place—the place that waits for me to fill it; to make my private self the means, my life the sphere and the function of the soul of the whole, which thus, personal in me, externalizes both itself and me into a solid reality, which is both mine and its.

(3) What we come to now is the third superiority of "my station and its duties." The universal which is the end, and which we have seen is concrete and does realize itself, does also more. It gets rid of the contradiction between duty and the "empirical" self; it does not in its realization leave me forever outside and unrealized.

In "duty for duty's sake" we were always unsatisfied, no nearer our goal at the end than at the beginning. There we had the fixed antithesis of the sensuous self on one side, and a nonsensuous moral ideal on the other—a standing contradiction which brought with it a perpetual self-deceit, or the depressing perpetual confession that I am not what I ought to be in my inner heart, and that I never can be so. Duty, we thus saw, was an infinite process, an unending "not-yet"; a continual "not" with an everlasting "to be," or an abiding "to be" with a ceaseless "not."

From this last peevish enemy we are again delivered by "my station and its duties." There I realize myself morally, so that not only what ought to be in the world is, but I am what I ought to be, and find so my contentment and satisfaction. If this were not the case, when we consider that the ordinary moral man is self-contented and happy, we should be forced to accuse him of immorality, and we do not do this; we say he most likely might be better, but we do not say that he is bad, or need consider himself so. Why is this? It is because "my station and its duties" teaches us to identify others and ourselves with the station we fill; to consider that as good, and by virtue of that to consider others and ourselves good too. It teaches us that a man who does his work in the world is good, notwithstanding his faults, if his faults do not prevent him from fulfilling his station. It tells us that the heart is an idle abstraction; we are not to think of it, nor must we look at our insides, but at our work and our life, and say to ourselves, Am I fulfilling my appointed function or not? Fulfill it we can, if we will. What we have to do is not so much better than the world that we cannot do it; the world is there waiting for it; my duties are my rights. On the one hand, I am not likely to be much better than the world asks me to be; on the other hand, if I can take my place in the world I ought not to be discontented. Here we must not be misunderstood; we do not say that the false self, the habits and desires opposed to the good will, are extinguished. Though negated, they never are all of them entirely suppressed, and cannot be. Hence we must not say that any man really does fill his station to the full height of his capacity; nor must we say of any man that he cannot perform his function better than he does, for we all can do so, and should try to do so. We do not wish to deny what are plain moral facts, nor in any way to slur them over.

How then does the contradiction disappear? It disappears by my identifying myself with the good will that I realize in the world, by my refusing to identify myself with the bad will of my private self. So far as I am one with the good will, living as a member in the moral organism, I am to consider myself real and I am not to consider the false self real. That cannot be attributed to me in my character of member in the organism. Even in me the false existence of it has been partly suppressed by that organism; and, so far as the organism is concerned, it is wholly suppressed because contradicted in its results, and allowed no reality. Hence, not existing for the organism, it does not exist for me as a member thereof; and only as a member thereof do I hold myself to be real. And yet this is not justification by faith, for we not only trust, but see, that despite our faults the moral world stands fast, and we in and by it. It is like faith, however, in this, that not merely by thinking ourselves, but by willing ourselves as such, can we look on ourselves as organs in a good whole, and so ourselves good. And further, the knowledge that as members of the system we are real, and not otherwise, encourages us more and more to identify ourselves with that system; to make ourselves better, and so more real, since we see that the good is real, and that nothing else is.

Or, to repeat it, in education my self by habituation has been growing into one with the good self around me, and by my free acceptance of my lot hereafter I consciously make myself one with the good, so that, though bad habits cling to and even arise in me, yet I cannot but be aware of myself as the reality of the good will. That is my essential side; my imperfections are not, and practically they do not matter. The good will in the world realizes itself by and in imperfect instruments, and in spite of them. The work is done, and so long as I will my part of the work and do it (as I do), I feel that, if I perform the function, I *am* the organ, and that my faults, if they do not matter to my station, do not matter to me. My heart I am not to think of, except to tell by my work whether it is in my work, and one with the moral whole; and if that is so, I have the consciousness of absolute reality in the good because of and by myself, and in myself because of and through the good; and with that I am satisfied, and have no right to be dissatisfied.

The individual's consciousness of himself is inseparable from the knowing himself as an organ of the whole; and the residuum falls more and more into the background, so that he thinks of it, if at all, not as himself, but as an idle appendage. For his nature now is not distinct from his "artificial self." He is related to the living moral system not as to a foreign body; his relation to it is "too inward even for faith," since faith implies a certain separation. It is no other-world that he cannot see but must trust to: he feels himself in it, and it in him; in a word, the self-consciousness of himself *is* the self-consciousness of the whole in him, and his will is the will which sees in him its accomplishment by him; it is the free will which knows itself as the free will, and as this beholds its realization and is more than content.

The non-theoretical person, if he be not immoral, is at peace with reality; and the man who in any degree has made this point of view his own becomes more and more reconciled to the world and to life, and the theories of "advanced thinkers" come to him more and more as the thinnest and most miserable abstractions. He sees evils which cannot discourage him, since they point to the strength of the life which can endure such parasites and flourish in spite of them. If the popularizing of superficial views inclines him to bitterness, he comforts himself when he sees that they live in the head, and but little, if at all, in the heart and life; that still at the push the doctrinaire and the quacksalver go to the wall, and that even that too is as it ought to be. He sees the true account of the state (which holds it to be neither mere force nor convention, but the moral organism, the real identity of might and right) unknown or "refuted," laughed at and despised, but he sees the state every day in its practice refute every other doctrine, and do with the moral approval of all what the explicit theory of scarcely one will morally justify. He sees instincts are better and stronger than so-called "principles." He sees in the hour of need what are called "rights" laughed at, "freedom," the liberty to do what one pleases, tramped on, the claims of the individual trodden under foot, and theories burst like cobwebs. And he sees, as of old, the heart of a nation rise high and beat in the breast of each one of her citizens till her safety and her honor are dearer to each than life, till to those who live her shame and sorrow, if such is allotted, outweigh their loss, and death seems a little thing to those who go for her to their common and nameless grave. And he knows that what is stronger than death is hate or love, hate here for love's sake, and that love does not fear death because already it is the death into life of what our philosophers tell us is the only life and reality.

Yes, the state is not put together, but it lives; it is not a heap nor a machine; it is no mere extravagance when a poet talks of a nation's soul. It is the objective mind which is subjective and self-conscious in its citizens—it feels and knows itself in the heart of each. It speaks the word of command and gives the field of accomplishment, and in the activity of obedience it has and bestows individual life and satisfaction and happiness.

First in the community is the individual realized. He is here the embodiment of beauty, goodness, and truth—of truth because he corresponds to his universal conception, of beauty because he realizes it in a single form to the senses or imagination, of goodness because his will expresses and is the will of the universal.

"The realm of morality is nothing but the absolute spiritual unity of the essence of individuals, which exists in the independent reality of them. . . . The moral substance, looked at abstractedly from the mere side of its universality, is the law, and, as this, is only thought; but nonetheless is it, from another point of view, immediate real self-consciousness or custom: and conversely the individual exists as this single unit, inasmuch as it is conscious in its individuality of the universal consciousness as its own being, inasmuch as its action and existence are the universal Ethos. . . They (the individuals) are aware in themselves that they possess this individual independent being because of the sacrifice of their individuality, because the universal substance is their soul and essence: and, on the other side, this universal is their individual action, the work that they as individuals have produced.

"The merely individual action and business of the separate person is concerned with the needs he is subject to as a natural being, as an individuality which exists. That even these his commonest functions do not come to nothing, but possess reality, is effected solely by the universal maintaining medium, by the power of the whole people. But it is not simply the form of persistence which the universal substance confers on his action; it gives also the content—what he does *is* the universal skill and custom of all. This content, just so far as it completely individualizes itself, is in its reality interlaced with the action of all. The work of the individual for his needs is a satisfaction of the needs of others as much as of his own; and he attains the satisfaction of his own only through the work of the others. The individual in his individual work thus accomplishes a universal work—he does so here *unconsciously*; but he also further accomplishes it as his *conscious* object: the whole as the whole is his work for which he sacrifices himself, and from which by that very sacrifice he gets again his self restored. Here there is nothing taken which is not given, nothing wherein the independent individual, by and in the resolution of his atomic existence, by and in the negation of his self, fails to give himself the positive significance of a being which exists by and for itself. The unity—on the one side of the being for another, or the making oneself into an outward thing, and on the other side of the being for oneself—this universal substance speaks its universal language in the usages and laws of his people: and yet this unchanging essence is itself nought else than the expression of the single individuality, which seems at first sight its mere opposite; the laws pronounce nothing but what everyone *is* and does. The individual recognizes the substance not only as his universal outward existence, but he recognizes also himself in it, particularized in his own individuality and in that of each of his fellow citizens. And so in the universal mind each one has nothing but self-certainty, the assurance of finding in existing reality nothing but himself. In all I contemplate independent beings, that are such, and are for themselves,

only in the very same way that I am for myself; in them I see
existing free unity of self with others, and existing by virtue of
me and by virtue of the others alike.   Them as myself, myself
as them.[5]

"In a free people, therefore, reason is realized in truth; it is
present living mind, and in this not only does the individual find
his destination, i. e., his universal and singular essence, promulgated and ready to his hand as an outward existence, but he himself is this essence, and has also reached and fulfilled his destination.   Hence the wisest men of antiquity have given judgment that
wisdom and virtue consist in living agreeably to the Ethos of one's
people."[6]

[5] Let me illustrate from our great poet:

> So they loved, as love in twain
> Had the essence but in one;
> Two distincts, division none:
> Number there in love was slain.
>
> Hearts remote yet not asunder;
> Distance, and no space was seen—
> So between them love did shine . . .
> Either was the other's mine.
>
> Property was thus appalled,
> That the self was not the same;
> Single nature's double name
> Neither two nor one was called.
>
> Reason, in itself confounded,
> Saw division grow together:
> To themselves yet either neither
> Simple were so well compounded,
>
> That it cried, How true a twain
> Seemeth this concordant one!
> Love hath reason, reason none,
> If what parts can so remain.
>   —(*The Phoenix and the Turtle*.)

Surely philosophy does not reach its end till the "reason of reason"
adequate to the "reason of love."

[6] Hegel, *Phänomenologie des Geistes* (1807), II, 256-8.

Once let us take the point of view which regards the community as the real moral organism, which in its members knows and wills itself and sees the individual to be real just so far as the universal self is in his self, as he in it, and we get the solution of most, if not all, of our previous difficulties. There is here no need to ask and by some scientific process find out what is moral, for morality exists all round us, and faces us, if need be, with a categorical imperative, while it surrounds us on the other side with an atmosphere of love.

The belief in this real moral organism is the one solution of ethical problems. It breaks down the antithesis of despotism and individualism; it denies them, while it preserves the truth of both. The truth of individualism is saved, because unless we have intense life and self-consciousness in the members of the state, the whole state is ossified. The truth of despotism is saved, because unless the member realizes the whole by and in himself, he fails to reach his own individuality. Considered in the main, the best communities are those which have the best men for their members, and the best men are the members of the best communities. Circle as this is, it is not a vicious circle. The two problems of the best man and best state are two sides, two distinguishable aspects of the one problem, how to realize in human nature the perfect unity of homogeneity and specification; and when we see that each of these without the other is unreal, then we see that (speaking in general) the welfare of the state and the welfare of its individuals are questions which it is mistaken and ruinous to separate. Personal morality and political and social institutions cannot exist apart, and (in general) the better the one the better the other. The community is moral because it realizes personal morality; personal morality is moral because and in so far as it realizes the moral whole.

It is here we find an answer to the complaint of our day on the dwindling of human nature. The higher the organism (we are told), the more are its functions specified, and hence narrowed. The man becomes a machine, or the piece of a machine; and, though the world grows, "the individual withers." On this we may first remark that, if what is meant is that the more centralized the system, the more narrow and monotonous is the life of the member, that is a very questionable assertion. If it be meant that the individual's life can be narrowed to "file-packing," or the like, without detriment to the intensity of the life of the whole, that is even more questionable. If again it be meant that in many cases we have a one-sided specification, which, despite the immediate stimulus of particular function implies ultimate loss of life to the body, that, I think, probably is so, but it is doubtful if we are compelled to think it always must be so. But the root of the whole complaint is a false view of things, which we have briefly noticed above (p. 23). The moral organism is not a mere animal organism. In the latter (it is no novel remark) the member is not aware of itself as such, while in the former it knows itself, and therefore knows the whole in itself. The narrow external function of the man is not the whole man. He has a life which we cannot see with our eyes; and there is no duty so mean that it is not the realization of this, and knowable as such. What counts is not the visible outer work so much as the spirit in which it is done. The breadth of my life is not measured by the multitude of my pursuits, nor the space I take up amongst other men, but by the fullness of the whole life which I know as mine. It is true that less now depends on each of us, as this or that man; it is not true that our individuality is therefore lessened, that therefore we have less in us.

Let us now consider our point of view in relation to certain antagonistic ideas; and first against the common error that there is something "right in itself" for me to do, in the sense that either there must be some absolute rule of morality the same for all persons without distinction of times and places, or else that all morality is "relative," and hence no morality. Let us begin by remarking that there is no such fixed code or rule of right. It is abundantly clear that the morality of one time is not that of another time, that the men considered good in one age might in another age not be thought good, that what would be right for us here might be mean and base in another country, and what would be wrong for us here might there be our bounden duty.

This is clear fact which is denied only in the interest of a foregone conclusion. The motive to deny it is the belief that it is fatal to morality. If what is right here is wrong there, then all morality (such is the notion) becomes chance and convention, and so ceases. But "my station and its duties" holds that *unless* morals varied, there could be no morality; that a morality which was *not* relative would be futile, and I should have to ask for something "more relative than this."

Let us explain. We hold that man is φύσει πολιτικός, that apart from the community he is θεὸς ἢ θήριον, no man at all. We hold again that the true nature of man, the oneness of homogeneity and specification, is being wrought out in history; in short, we believe in evolution. The process of evolution is the humanizing of the bestial foundation of man's nature by carrying out in it the true idea of man—in other words, by realizing man as an infinite whole (p. 18). This realization is possible only by the individual's living as member in a higher life, and this higher life is slowly developed in a series of stages. Starting from and on the basis of animal nature, humanity has worked itself out by gradual advances of specification and systematization, and any other progress would, in the world we know, have been impossible. The notion that full-fledged moral ideas fell down from heaven is contrary to all the facts with which we are acquainted. If they had done so, it would have been for their own sake; for by us they certainly could not have been perceived, much less applied. At any given period to know more than he did, man must have been more than he was; for a human being is nothing if he is not the son of his time, and he must realize himself as that, or he will not do it at all.

Morality is "relative," but is nonetheless real. At every stage there is the solid fact of a world so far moralized. There is an objective morality in the accomplished will of the past and present, a higher self worked out by the infinite pain, the sweat and blood of generations, and now given to me by free grace and in love and faith as a sacred trust. It comes to me as the truth of my own nature, and the power and the law, which is stronger and higher than any caprice or opinion of my own.

"Evolution," in this sense of the word, gives us over neither to chance nor alien necessity, for it is that self-realization which is the progressive conquest of both. But, on another understanding of the term, we cannot help asking, Is this still the case, and is "my station" a tenable point of view?

Wholly tenable, in the form in which we have stated it, it is not. For if, in saying Morality has developed, all we mean is that something has happened different from earlier events, that human society has changed, and that the alterations, so far as we know them, are more or less of a certain sort; if "progress" signifies that an advance has been set going and is kept up by chance in an unknown direction; that the higher is, in short, what *is* and what before was not, and that what will be, of whatever sort it is, will still be a step in progress; if, in short, the movement of history toward a goal is mere illusion, and the stages of that movement are nothing but the successes of what from time to time somehow happens to be best suited to the chance of circumstances—then it is clear in the first place that, teleology being banished, such words as evolution[7] and progress have lost their own meaning, and that to speak of humanity realizing itself in history, and of myself finding in that movement the truth of myself worked out, would be simply to delude oneself with hollow phrases.

Thus far we must say that on such a view of "development"

[7] With respect to "evolution" I may remark in passing that, though this word may of course be used to stand for anything whatever, yet for all that it has a meaning of its own, which those who care to use words, not merely with *a* meaning, but also with *their* meaning, would do well to consider. To try to exhibit all that is contained in it would be a serious matter, but we may call attention to a part. And first, "evolution," "development," "progress," all imply something identical throughout, a subject of the evolution, which is one and the same. If what is there at the beginning is not there at the end, and the same as what was there at the beginning, then evolution is a word with no meaning. Something must evolve itself, and that something, which is the end, must also be the beginning. It must be what moves itself to the end, and must be the end which is the "because" of the motion. Evolution must evolve itself to itself, progress itself go forward to a goal which is itself, development bring out nothing but what was in, and bring it out, not from external compulsion, but *because* it is in.

the doctrine of "my station" is grievously curtailed. But is it destroyed? Not wholly; though sorely mutilated, it still keeps its ground. We have rejected teleology but have not yet embraced individualism. We still believe that the universal self is more than a collection or an idea, that it is reality, and that apart from it the "individuals" are the fictions of a theory. We have still the fact of the one self particularized in its many members; and the right and duty of gaining self-realization through the real universal is still as certain as is the impossibility of gaining it otherwise. And so "my station" is after all a position, not indeed satisfactory, but not yet untenable.

But if the larger doctrine be the truth, if evolution is more than a tortured phrase, and progress to a goal no mere idea but an actual fact, then history is the working out of the true human nature through various incomplete stages toward completion, and "my station" is the one satisfactory view of morals. Here (as we have seen) all morality is and must be "relative" because the essence of realization is evolution through stages, and hence existence in some one stage which is not final; here, on the other hand, all morality is "absolute" because in every stage the essence of man *is* realized, however imperfectly; and yet again the distinction of right in itself against relative morality is not banished, because, from the point of view of a higher stage, we can see that lower stages failed to realize the truth completely enough, and also, mixed and one with their realization, did present features contrary to the true nature of man as we now see it. Yet herein the

And further, unless what is at the end is different from that which was at the beginning, there is no evolution. That which develops, or evolves itself, both is and is not. It *is,* or it could not be *it* which develops, and which at the end has developed. It *is not,* or else it could not become. It becomes what it is; and, if this is nonsense, then evolution is nonsense.

Evolution is a contradiction; and, when the contradiction ceases, the evolution ceases. The process is a contradiction, and only *because* it is a contradiction can it be a process. So long as progress lasts, contradiction lasts; so long as anything becomes, it is not. To be realized is to cease to progress. To be at the end (in one sense) is to lose the end (in another), and that because (in both senses) all then comes to the end. For the process is a contradiction, and the solution of the contradiction is in every sense the *end* of the process.

morality of every stage is justified for that stage; and the demand for a code of right in itself, apart from any stage, is seen to be the asking for an impossibility.

The next point we come to is the question, How do I get to know in particular what is right and wrong? and here again we find a strangely erroneous preconception. It is thought that moral philosophy has to accomplish this task for us, and the conclusion lies near at hand that any system which will not do this is worthless. Well, we first remark, and with some confidence, that there cannot be a moral philosophy which will tell us what in particular we are to do, and also that it is not the business of philosophy to do so. All philosophy has to do is "to understand what is," and moral philosophy has to understand morals which exist, not to make them or give directions for making them. Such a notion is simply ludicrous. Philosophy in general has not to anticipate the discoveries of the particular sciences nor the evolution of history; the philosophy of religion has not to make a new religion or teach an old one, but simply to understand the religious consciousness; and aesthetic has not to produce works of fine art, but to theorize the beautiful which it finds; political philosophy has not to play tricks with the state, but to understand it; and ethics has not to make the world moral, but to reduce to theory the morality current in the world. If we want it to do anything more, so much the worse for us; for it cannot possibly construct new morality, and, even if it could to any extent codify what exists (a point on which I do not enter), yet it surely is clear that in cases of collision of duties it would not help you to know what to do. Who would go to a learned theologian, as such, in a practical religious difficulty; to a system of aesthetic for suggestions on the handling of an artistic theme; to a physiologist, as such, for a diagnosis and prescription; to a political philosopher in practical politics; or to a psychologist in an intrigue of any kind? All these persons no doubt *might* be the best to go to, but that would not be because they were the best theorists, but because they were more. In short, the view which thinks moral philosophy is to supply us with particular moral prescriptions confuses science with art, and confuses, besides, reflective with intuitive judgment. That which tells us what in particular is right and wrong is not reflection but intuition.[8]

We know what is right in a particular case by what we may call an immediate judgment, or an intuitive subsumption. These phrases are perhaps not very luminous, and the matter of the "intuitive understanding" in general is doubtless difficult, and the special character of moral judgments not easy to define; and I do not say that I am in a position to explain these subjects at all, nor, I think, could anyone do so, except at considerable length. But the point that I do wish to establish here is, I think, not at all obscure. The reader has first to recognize that moral judgments are not discursive; next, that nevertheless they do start from and rest on a certain basis; and then if he puts the two together, he will see that they involve what he may call the "intuitive under-standing," or any other name, so long as he keeps in sight the two elements and holds them together.

On the head that moral judgments are not discursive, no one, I think, will wish me to stay long. If the reader attends to the facts he will not want anything else; and if he does not, I confess I cannot prove my point. In practical morality, no doubt, we *may* reflect on our principles, but I think it is not too much to say that we *never* do so, except where we have come upon a difficulty of particular application. If anyone thinks that a man's *ordinary* judgment, "this is right or wrong," comes from the having a rule *before* the mind and bringing the particular case under it, he may be right, and I cannot try to show that he is wrong. I can only leave it to the reader to judge for himself. We say we "see" and we "feel" in these cases, not we "conclude." We prize the advice of persons who can give us no reasons for what they say. There is a general belief that the having a reason for all your actions is

---

[8] I must ask the reader here not to think of "Intuitionalism," or of "Organs of the Absolute," or of anything else of the sort. "Intuitive" is used here as the opposite of "reflective" or "discursive"; "intuition" as the opposite of "reasoning" or "explicit inferring." If the reader dislike the word, he may substitute "perception" or "sense," if he will; but then he must remember that neither are to exclude the intellectual, the understanding and its implicit judgments and inferences.

pedantic and absurd. There is a general belief that to try t
have reasons for all that you do is sometimes very dangerou
Not only the woman but the man who deliberates may be los
First thoughts are often the best,[9] and if once you begin to argu
with the devil you are in a perilous state. And I think I ma
add (though I do it in fear) that women are remarkable for th
fineness of their moral perceptions[10] and the quickness of thei
judgments, and yet are or (let me save myself by saying) "ma
be" not remarkable for corresponding discursive ability.

Taking for granted then that our ordinary way of judging i
morals is not by reflection and explicit reasoning, we have no
to point to the other side of the fact, viz., that these judgmen
are not mere isolated impressions, but stand in an intimate an
vital relation to a certain system, which is their basis. Her
again we must ask the reader to pause, if in doubt, and conside
the facts for himself. Different men, who have lived in differen
times and countries, judge a fresh case in morals differently
Why is this? There is probably no "why" before the mind o
either when he judges; but *we* perhaps can say, "I know why A
said so and B so," because we find some general rule or princip
different in each, and in each the basis of the judgment. Differen
people in the same society may judge points differently, and w
sometimes know why. It is because A is struck by one aspec
of the case, B by another; and one principle is (not *before*, but
in A's mind when he judges, and another in B's. Each ha
subsumed, but under a different head; the one perhaps justice
the other gratitude. Every man has the morality he has mad
his own in his mind, and he "sees" or "feels" or "judges" accord
ingly, though he does not reason explicitly from data to a con
clusion.

I think this will be clear to the reader; and so we must sa

[9] It is right to remark that second thoughts are often the offspring o
wrong desire, but not always so. They may arise from collisions, and i
these cases we see how little is to be done by theoretical deduction.

[10] Not, perhaps, on *all* matters. Nor, again, will it do to say that *every
where* women are pre-eminently intuitive, and men discursive. But i
practical matters there seems not much doubt that it is so.

that on their perceptive or intellectual side (and that, the reader must not forget, is the one side that we are considering) our moral judgments are intuitive subsumptions.

To the question, How am I to know what is right? the answer must be, By the αἴσθησις of the φρόνιμος; and the φρόνιμος is the man who has identified his will with the moral spirit of the community, and judges accordingly. If an immoral course be suggested to him, he "feels" or "sees" at once that the act is not in harmony with a good will, and he does not do this by saying, "this is a breach of rule A, *therefore*, etc.," but the first thing he is aware of is that he "does not like it"; and what he has done, without being aware of it, is (at least in most cases) to seize the quality of the act, that quality being a general quality. Actions of a particular kind he does not like, and he has instinctively referred the particular act to that kind. What is right is perceived in the same way; courses suggest themselves, and one is approved of, because intuitively judged to be of a certain kind, which kind represents a principle of the good will.

If a man is to know what is right, he should have imbibed by precept, and still more by example, the spirit of his community, its general and special beliefs as to right and wrong, and, with this whole embodied in his mind should particularize it in any new case, not by a reflective deduction, but by an intuitive subsumption, which does not know that it is a subsumption;[11] by a

---

[11] Every act has, of course, many sides, many relations, many "points of view from which it may be regarded," and so many qualities. There are always several principles under which you can bring it, and hence there is not the smallest difficulty in exhibiting it as the realization of either right or wrong. No act in the world is without *some* side capable of being subsumed under a good rule, *e. g.*, theft is economy, care for one's relations, protest against bad institutions, really doing oneself but justice, etc.; and, if all else fails, it probably saves us from something worse, and therefore is good. Cowardice is prudence and a duty, courage rashness and a vice, and so on. The casuist must have little ingenuity, if there is anything he fails to justify or condemn according to his order. And the vice of casuistry is that, attempting to decide the particulars of morality by the deductions of the reflective understanding, it at once degenerates into finding a good reason for what you mean to do. You have principles of all sorts, and the case has all sorts of sides; *which* side is the essential side, and which principle is *the*

carrying out of the self into a new case, wherein what is before the mind is the case and not the self to be carried out, and where it is indeed the whole that feels and sees, but all that is seen is seen in the form of *this* case, *this* point, *this* instance. Precept is good, but example is better; for by a series of particulars (as such forgotten) we get the general spirit, we identify ourselves both on the side of will and judgment with the basis, which basis (be it remembered) has not got to be explicit.[12]

principle *here*, rests in the end on your mere private choice, and that is determined by heaven knows what. No *reasoning* will tell you which the moral point of view *here* is. Hence the necessary immorality and the ruinous effects of practical casuistry. (Casuistry used not as a guide to conduct, but as a means to the theoretical investigation of moral principles, the casuistry used to discover the principle *from* the fact, and not to deduce the fact from the principle—is, of course, quite another thing.) Our moralists do not like casuistry; but if the current notion that moral philosophy has to tell you what to do is well founded, then casuistry, so far as I can see, at once follows, or should follow.

But the ordinary moral judgment is not discursive. It does not look to the right and left, and, considering the case from all its sides, consciously subsume under one principle. When the case is presented, it fixes on one quality in the act, referring that unconsciously to one principle in which it feels the whole of itself, and sees that whole in a single side of the act. So far as right and wrong are concerned it can perceive nothing but *this* quality of *this* case, and anything else it refuses to try to perceive. Practical morality means single-mindedness, the having one idea; it means what in other spheres would be the greatest narrowness. Point out to a man of simple morals that the case has other sides than the one he instinctively fixes on and he suspects you wish to corrupt him. And so you probably would if you went on. Apart from bad example, the readiest way to debauch the morality of any one is, on the side of principle, to confuse them by forcing them to see in all moral and immoral acts other sides and points of view, which alter the character of each; and, on the side of particulars, to warp their instinctive apprehension through personal affection for yourself or some other individual.

[12] It is worth while in this connection to refer to the custom some persons have (and find useful) of calling before the mind, when in doubt, a known person of high character and quick judgment, and thinking what they would have done. This no doubt both delivers the mind from private considerations and also is to act in the spirit of the other person (so far as we know it), *i. e.*, from the general basis of his acts (certainly *not* the mere memory of his particular acts, or such memory plus inference).

There are a number of questions which invite considerations[13] here, but we cannot stop. We wished to point out briefly the character of our common moral judgments. This (on the intellectual side) is the way in which they are ordinarily made; and, in the main, there is not much practical difficulty. What is moral *in any particular given case* is seldom doubtful. Society pronounces beforehand; or, after some one course has been taken, it can say whether it was right or not; though society cannot generalize much, and, if asked to reflect, is helpless and becomes incoherent. But I do not say there are no cases where the morally minded man has to doubt; most certainly such do arise, though not so many as some people think, far fewer than some would be glad to think. A very large number arise from reflection, which wants to act from an explicit principle, and so begins to abstract and divide, and, thus becoming one-sided, makes the relative absolute. Apart from this, however, collisions must take place, and here there is no guide whatever but the intuitive judgment of oneself or others.[14]

This intuition must not be confounded with what is sometimes miscalled "conscience." It is not mere individual opinion or caprice. It presupposes the morality of the community as its basis, and is subject to the approval thereof. Here, if anywhere, the idea of universal and impersonal morality is realized. For the final arbiters are the φρόνιμοι, persons with a will to do right, and not full of reflections and theories. If they fail you, you must judge for yourself, but practically they seldom do fail you. Their private peculiarities neutralize each other, and the result is an intuition which does not belong merely to this or that man or collection of men. "Conscience" is the antipodes of this. It wants you to have no law but yourself, and to be better than the world. But this tells you that, if you could be as good as your

---

[13] One of these would be as to how progress in morality is made.

[14] I may remark on this (after Erdmann, and I suppose Plato) that collisions of duties are avoided mostly by each man keeping to his own immediate duties, and not trying to see from the point of view of other stations than his own.

world, you would be better than most likely you are, and that to wish to be better than the world is to be already on the threshold of immorality.

This perhaps "is a hard saying," but it is least hard to those who know life best; it is intolerable to those mainly who, from inexperience or preconceived theories, cannot see the world as it is. Explained it may be by saying that enthusiasm for good dies away—the ideal fades:

> Dem Herrlichsten, was auch der Geist empfangen,
> Drängt immer fremd und fremder Stoff sich an;

but better perhaps if we say that those who have seen most of the world (not one side of it)—old people of no one-sided profession nor of immoral life—know most also how much good there is in it. They are tolerant of new theories and youthful opinions that everything would be better upside down because they know that this also is as it should be, and that the world gets good even from these. They are intolerant only of those who are old enough, and should be wise enough, to know better than that they know better than the world; for in such people they cannot help seeing the self-conceit which is pardonable only in youth.

Let us be clear. What is that wish to be better, and to make the world better, which is on the threshold of immorality? What is the "world" in this sense? It is the morality already existing ready to hand in laws, institutions, social usages, moral opinions and feelings. This is the element in which the young are brought up. It has given moral content to themselves and it is the only source of such content. It is not wrong, it is a duty, to take the best that there is, and to live up to the best. It is not wrong, it is a duty, standing on the basis of the existing, and in harmony with its general spirit, to try and make not only oneself but also the world better, or rather, and in preference, one's own world better. But it is another thing, starting from oneself, from ideals in one's head, to set oneself and them against the moral world. The moral world with its social institutions, etc., is a fact; it is real; our "ideals" are not real. "But we will make them real."

We should consider what we are, and what the world is. We should learn to see the great moral fact in the world, and to reflect on the likelihood of our private "ideal" being anything more than an abstraction, which, because an abstraction, is all the better fitted for our heads, and all the worse fitted for actual existence.

We should consider whether the encouraging oneself in having opinions of one's own, in the sense of thinking differently from the world on moral subjects, be not, in any person other than a heaven-born prophet, sheer self-conceit. And though the disease may spend itself in the harmless and even entertaining sillinesses by which we are advised to assert our social "individuality," yet still the having theories of one's own in the face of the world is not far from having practice in the same direction; and if the latter is (as it often must be) immorality, the former has certainly but stopped at the threshold.

But the moral organism is strong against both. The person anxious to throw off the yoke of custom and develop his "individuality" in startling directions, passes as a rule into the common Philistine, and learns that Philistinism is after all a good thing. And the licentious young man, anxious for pleasure at any price, who, without troubling himself about "principles," does put into practice the principles of the former person, finds after all that the self within him can be satisfied only with that from whence it came. And some fine morning the dream is gone, the enchanted bower is a hideous phantasm, and the despised and common reality has become the ideal.

We have thus seen the community to be the real moral idea, to be stronger than the theories and the practice of its members against it, and to give us self-realization. And this is indeed limitation; it bids us say farewell to visions of superhuman morality, to ideal societies, and to practical "ideals" generally. But perhaps the unlimited is not the perfect nor the true ideal. And, leaving "ideals" out of sight, it is quite clear that if anybody wants to realize himself as a perfect man without trying to be a perfect member of his country and all his smaller communities, he makes what all sane persons would admit to be a great mistake. There is no more fatal enemy than theories which are not also facts; and when people inveigh against the vulgar antithesis of the two, they themselves should accept their own doctrine, and give up the harboring of theories of what should be and is not. Until they do that, the vulgar are in the right; for a theory of that which (only) is to be, is a theory of that which in fact is not, and that I suppose is only a theory.

There is nothing better than my station and its duties, nor anything higher or more truly beautiful. It holds and will hold its own against the worship of the "individual," whatever form that may take. It is strong against frantic theories and vehement passions, and in the end it triumphs over the fact and can smile at the literature, even of sentimentalism, however fulsome in its impulsive setting out, or sour in its disappointed end. It laughs at its frenzied apotheosis of the yet unsatisfied passion it calls love; and at that embitterment too which has lost its illusions, and yet cannot let them go—with its kindness for the genius too clever in general to do anything in particular, and its adoration of star-gazing virgins with souls above their spheres, whose wish to be something in the world takes the form of wanting to do something with it, and who in the end do badly what they might have done in the beginning well; and, worse than all, its cynical contempt for what deserves only pity, sacrifice of a life for work to the best of one's lights, a sacrifice despised not simply because it has failed, but because it is stupid, and uninteresting, and altogether unsentimental.

And all these books (ah! how many) it puts into the one scale, and with them the writers of them; and into the other scale it puts three such lines as these:

> "One place performs like any other place
> The proper service every place on earth
> Was framed to furnish man with" ——
> κόκκυ, μεθεῖτε· καὶ πολύ γε κατωτέρω
> χωρεῖ τὸ τοῦδε,

> Have we still to ask,
> καὶ τί ποτ᾽ ἐστὶ ταἴτιον;[15]

[15] Arist. *Frogs*, 1384. *Dionysos*—Cuckoo! Let go the scales; Aeschylos'

The theory which we have just exhibited (more or less in our own way), and over which perhaps we have heated ourselves a little, seems to us a great advance on anything we have had before, and indeed in the main to be satisfactory. It satisfies us because in it our wills attain their realization; the content of the will is a whole, is systematic; and it is the same whole on both sides. On the outside and inside alike we have the same universal will in union with the particular personality; and in the identity of inside and outside in one single process we have reached the point where the "is to be," with all its contradictions, disappears, or remains but as a moment in a higher "is."

Nonetheless, however, must we consider this satisfaction neither ultimate, nor all-inclusive, nor anything but precarious. If put forth as that beyond which we do not need to go, as the end in itself, it is open to very serious objections, some of which we must now develop.

The point upon which "my station and its duties" prided itself most, was that it had got rid of the opposition of "ought" and "is" in both its forms; viz., the opposition of the outer world to the "ought" in me, and the opposition of my particular self to the "ought" in general. We shall have to see that it has not succeeded in doing either, or at least not completely.

(1) Within the sphere of my station and its duties the opposition is not vanquished; for:

(a) It is impossible to maintain the doctrine of what may be called "justification by sight." The self cannot be so seen to be identified with the moral whole that the bad self disappears. (i) In the moral man the consciousness of that unity cannot be present always, but only when he is fully engaged in satisfactory work. Then, I think, it is present; but when he is not so engaged, and the bad self shows itself, he can scarcely be self-contented, or, if he is so, scarcely because he *sees* that the bad self is unreal. He can only forget his faults when he is too busy to think of them; and he can hardly be so always. And he can not always *see* that his faults do not matter to the moral order of

side goes down, oh, much much the lowest. *Euripides*—Why, what ever is the reason?

things—when it comes to that he can only trust. Further, (ii) the more or less immoral man who, because of past offenses, is now *unable* to perform his due function, or to perform it duly, cannot always in his work gain once more the self-content he has lost because that very work tells him of what should have been, and now is not and will not be, and the habits he has formed perhaps drag him still into the faults that made them. We cannot, without taking a low point of view, ask that this man's life, morally considered, should be more than a struggle; and it would be the most untrue Pharisaism or indifferentism to call him immoral because he struggles, and so far as he struggles. Here justification by sight is out of the question.

(b) Again, the moral man need not find himself realized in the world. (i) It is necessary to remark that the community in which he is a member may be in a confused or rotten condition, so that in it right and might do not always go together. And (ii) the very best community can only insure that correspondence in the gross; it cannot do so in every single detail. (iii) There are afflictions for which no moral organism has balm or physician, though it has alleviation; and these can mar the life of any man. (iv) The member may have to sacrifice himself for the community. In none of these cases can he *see* his realization; and here again the contradiction breaks out, and we must wrap ourselves in a virtue which is our own and not the world's, or seek a higher doctrine by which, through faith and through faith alone, self-suppression issues in a higher self-realization.

(2) Within the sphere of my station and its duties we see the contradiction is but partially solved, and the second objection is also very serious. You cannot confine a man to his station and its duties. Whether in another sense that formula would be all-embracing is a further question, but in the sense in which we took it, function in a "visible" community, it certainly is not so. And we must remark here in passing that, if we accept (as I think we must) the fact that the essence of a man involves identity with others, the question what the final reality of that identity is, is still left unanswered. We should still have to ask what is the higher whole in which the individual is a function, and in which

the relative wholes subsist, and to inquire whether that community is, or can be, a visible community at all.

Passing by this, however, let us develop our objection. A man cannot take his morality simply from the moral world he is in, for many reasons. (a) That moral world, being in a state of historical development, is not and cannot be self-consistent; and the man must thus stand before and above inconsistencies and reflect on them. This must lead to the knowledge that the world is not altogether as it should be, and to a process of trying to make it better. With this cooperates (b) what may be called cosmopolitan morality. Men nowadays know to some extent what is thought right and wrong in other communities now, and what has been thought at other times; and this leads to a notion of goodness not of any particular time and country. For numbers of persons no doubt this is unnecessary; but it is necessary for others, and they have the moral ideal (with the psychological origin of which we are not concerned) of a good man who is not good as member of this or that community, but who realizes himself in whatever community he finds himself. This, however, must mean also that he is not perfectly realized in any particular station.

(3) We have seen that the moral man can to a certain extent distinguish his moral essence from his particular function; and now a third objection at once follows, that the content of the ideal self does not fall wholly within any community, is in short *not* merely the ideal of a perfect social being. The making myself better does not always directly involve relation to others. The production of truth and beauty (together with what is called "culture") may be recognized as a duty; and it will be very hard to reduce it in all cases to a duty of any station that I can see. If we like to say that these duties to myself are duties to humanity, that perhaps is true; but we must remember that humanity is not a visible community. If you mean by it only past, present, and future human beings, then you cannot show that in all cases my culture is of use (directly or indirectly) to anyone but myself. Unless you are prepared to restrict science and fine art to what is useful, *i. e.*, to common arts and "accomplishments," you cannot hope to "verify" such an assertion. You are in the region of belief,

not knowledge; and this equally whether your belief is true or false. We must say then that, in aiming at truth and beauty, we are trying to realize ourself not as a member of any visible community.

And, finally, against this ideal self the particular person remains and must remain imperfect. The ideal self is not fully realized in us, in any way that we can see. We are aware of a ceaseless process, it is well if we can add progress, in which the false private self is constantly subdued but never disappears. And it never can disappear—we are never realized. The contradiction remains; and not to feel it demands something lower or something higher than a moral point of view.

Starting from these objections, our next Essay must try to make more clear what is involved in them, and to raise in a sharper form the difficulties as to the nature of morality. And our Concluding Remarks will again take up the same thread, after we have in some measure investigated in Essay VII the difficult problems of the bad self and selfishness.

NOTE

RIGHTS AND DUTIES

To handle this subject properly, more space would be wanted than I have at command. But I will make some remarks shortly and in outline.

A great to-do has been made about the ambiguity of the word "right"; as I think, needlessly. Right is the rule, and what is conformable to the rule, whether that rule be physical or mental; *e. g.*, a right line, a "right English bull-dog" (Swift), a right conclusion, a right action.

Right is, generally, the expression of the universal. It is the emphasis of the universal side in the relation of particular and universal. It implies particulars, and therefore possibility of discrepancy between them and the universal. Hence right means law; which law may be carried out or merely stated. "Is it right to do this?" means "is the universal realized in this?" "Have I a right?" means "am I in this the expression of law?"

In the moral sphere, with which alone we are concerned, right means always the relation of the universal to the particular will. The emphasis is on the universal. Possibility of discrepancy with a conscious subject makes law here *command*.

Command is the simple proposal of an action (or abstinence) to me by another will, as the content of that will. Or, from the side of the commander, it is the willing by me of some state of another will, such willing being presented by me as a fact to that will. Threat is not of the essence of command; command need not imply the holding forth or the anticipation of consequences.

To *have* rights is not merely to be the object with respect to which commands (positive or prohibitory) are addressed to others. If that were so, inanimate matter would have rights; *e. g.*, the very dirt in the road would "have a right" to be taken up or let lie— and this is barbarous. To have rights is to be (or to be presumed to be) capable of realizing the universal command consciously as such.[1] This answers the question, Has a beast rights? He is the object of duties, not the subject of rights. Right is the universal in its relation to a will capable of recognizing it as such, whether it remain mere command or is also carried out in act.

Wherever in the moral world you have law you have also right and rights. These may be real or ideal. The first are the will of the state or society, the second the will of the ideal-social or nonsocial ideal. (*Vide* Essay VI.)

It is in order to secure the existence of right in the acts of particular wills that compulsion is used. But compulsion is not necessary to the general and abstract definition of right, and it cannot be immediately deduced from it.

---

[1] "I have rights against others," or "I have a right to this or that from others," means, (1) it is right, it is the expression of the universal that they should do this or that in reference to me: I am the object of their duty. But this by itself does not give me "rights." To "have a right" to anything from another, I must (2) be a subject which knows the universal as such, both (a) in its *immediate* relation to my will, in its expression through my acts; and (b) also here in its expression through the acts of others, which acts may concern me. When my will as the universal, and the universal as my will, calls for these acts, then I "have a right" to them in the proper sense, but not otherwise.

What is duty? It is simply the other side of right. It is the same relation, viewed from the other pole or moment. It is the relation of the particular to the universal, with the emphasis on the particular. It is *my* will in its affirmative relation to the objective will. Right is the universal, existing for thought alone or also carried out. Duty is my will, either merely thought of as realizing this universal, or actually also doing so. "This is my duty" means "in this I identify, or am thought of as identifying, myself with right."

Duty, like right, implies possible discordance of particular and universal. Like right, too, it implies more than this. It implies the consciousness (or presumed capacity for consciousness) of the relation of my will to the universal as the right. Hence a beast has no duties in the proper sense. If he has, then he has also rights.

Right is the universal will implying particular will. It is the objective side implying a subjective side, *i. e.*, duty. Duty is the particular will implying a universal will. It is the subjective side implying an objective side, *i. e.*, right. But the two sides are inseparable. No right without duty; no duty without right and rights. (To this we shall return.)

Right and duty are sides of a single whole. This whole is the good. Rights and duties imply the identity, and nonidentity, of the particular and universal wills. Right may remain a mere command, duty a mere "ought to be," the nonagreement of the particular and universal. They are both abstractions. They are both, if fixed and isolated one from the other, self-contradictions. Each by itself is a mere "is to be," each a willed idea, which, so long as apart from the other, remains a *mere*, *i. e.*, a *not*-willed idea. Each is a single side of one and the same relation, fixed apart from the other side. In the good the sides come together, and in the whole first cease to be abstractions and gain real existence. The right is carried out in duty. The duty realizes itself in the right.

But in the good rights and duties as such disappear. There is no more mere right or mere duty, no more particular and universal as such, no external relation of the two. They are now sides and elements in one whole; and, if they appear, it is only as, within the movement and life of the whole, here one element and there another has its relative emphasis. But outside the whole their reality fades into "mere idea," into legend and fable.

Rights and duties do not exist outside the moral world; and that world does not exist where there is not a sphere of inner morality, however immediate, the consciousness, however vague, of the relation of the private will to the universal, whether that universal be presented as outer (in the shape of tribal custom or of some individual) or again as inner. Where there is no morality there is no right; where there is no right there are no rights. Just so, where there are no rights there is no right, and where no right there no morality. Inner morality without an objective right and wrong is a self-delusion. Right and rights outside morality are a mere fiction.

It is here that every partial theory of morals and politics is wrecked and seen to be worthless. False theories of right either (1) fail to get to any objective universal except by some fond invention (of contract), which, besides being an invention, presupposes what it is to create. (A contract outside the sphere of right and morality is nonsense.) Or (2) they take an objective universal (as positive law, will of the monarch, or what seems most convenient to the majority); and here they fail because their right is mere force, and is not moral, not right at all; and hence they cannot show that I am *in* the right to obey it, or in the wrong to disobey it, but merely that, if I do not obey it, it may (or may not) be inconvenient for me. So again in morals they either (1) posit a universal, such as the will of the Deity or of other human beings; and this fails because in it I do not affirm *my* self; or else (2) there is nothing anywhere objective and universal at all; and here I affirm nothing *but* myself. In either case there is no duty and no morality.

"But rights and duties," we shall be told, "collide." They collide only as rights do with rights or duties with duties. Rights and duties of one sphere collide with those of another sphere, and again within each sphere they collide in different persons, and again in one and the same person. But that right as such can collide with duty as such is impossible. There is no right which is not a duty, no duty which is not a right. In either case right would cease to be right, and duty duty.

This will be denied. It will be said, (1) there are duties without rights; (2) rights without duties. As to the first (1) we say, If we have not a right to do anything, it is not right for us. If it is not right for us, then it is not our duty. It is quite true that *moral* duty may not be *legal* right, nor *legal* duty *moral* right, but this is not to the point.

As to the second (2), it seems harder to see that where I have no duties I have no rights. In the spheres of the state, of society, of ideal morality, I have a right to do this and not that, that and not the other. But can it be said that all these things that I have a right to do are my duties? Is not that nonsense?

No doubt there is much truth in this. It is almost as bad to have nothing *but* duties as it is to have no duties at all. For free individual self-development we must have both elements. Where the universal is all there is ossification; where the particular is all there is dissolution; in neither case life.

Is it true then that there are rights where there are no duties? No. In a sense, rights are wider than duties: but what does this mean? Does it mean there are rights outside the moral sphere? Certainly not. We shall see (Essay VI) that there is no limit to the moral sphere; and if there were a limit, then outside that rights would cease to be rights. "More rights than duties" then must be true, if at all, *within* the moral sphere. Does it hold there that there are more rights than duties? It is not a very hard puzzle. To make it easier let us double it, and say "there are more duties than rights." A man, for instance, has a certain indivisible sum to spend in charity. He has a duty to A, B, and C, but not a right to more than one because it is wrong if he gives more than his indivisible limited sum. Hence there are more duties than rights. All that it comes to is that, when you look on duties as possible, they are wider than what, when actually done, is right and actual duty. Just so possible rights are wider than what is actually duty and actually right.

The reason why this is noticed on the side of rights, and not on the side of duty, is very simple. We saw above that in right the emphasis is on the universal side. Now every act is a determined this or that act, and what makes it a this or that act is the particularization. What I have a right to do thus depends on what my duty is; for duty, we saw, emphasized the particular side. Now, where there are no indifferents and no choice between them, rights are never wider than duties. It is where indifferents come in (cf. Essay VI), that possibility is wider than actuality. And because right emphasizes the side common to all the indifferents, *i. e.*, the undetermined side, it is therefore wider than duty, which emphasizes the particular side, and hence is narrower.

Thus, where the choice of my particular will comes in, that has rights and must be respected. But it has rights only because the sphere of its exercise, and therefore what it does therein, is duty. And it must be respected by others only so far as it thus expresses the universal will. If it has not right on its side, it has no rights whatever.

There is indeed a sphere where rights seem in collision with right. Wherever you have law you have this, since it comes from the nature of law. Thus I am *just*ified in returning evil for evil; I have a right to do it, even where it is not right but wrong to do it. The same thing is found in the spheres of state law, social law, and mere moral law alike. This does not show that in these cases there is *no* moral universal; it shows that we are keeping to nothing *but* the universal. We have here the distinction of justice and equity. A merely just[2] act may (we all know) be most unjust. The universal as law must be the same for all: it cannot be specified to meet every particular case. Hence, in keeping to this unspecified universal, I have "right" on my side; but again, failing to specify it in my case, I do what is not right for me to do. I fail in duty, do not do, and am not, right.

The sphere of mere private right in the state cannot exist out

[2] What is justice? I have no space to develop or illustrate, but will set down what seems to be the fact. The just does not = right; injustice does not = wrong. Justice does not = giving to each deserts: "nothing but justice" may be less or more than my deserts. Justice is not *mere* conforming to law; injustice is not *mere* acting against law; *e. g.*, murder is not

of the moral whole. It is, for the sake of the development of the whole, created and kept up in the whole, but merely at the pleasure of the whole. Just so in morals there is a sphere of private liking, the sphere of indifferents, but this exists only because it ought to exist, only because duty is realized in its existence, though not by its particulars as particulars, *i. e.*, as this one against that one. The sphere of private right has rights only so long as it is right and is duty. It exists merely on sufferance; and the moment the right of the whole demands its suppression it has no rights. Public right everywhere overrides it in practice, if not in theory. This is the justification of such things as forcible expropriation, conscription, etc. The only proper way of regarding them is to say, In developing my property, etc., as this or that man, I am doing my duty to the state, for the state lives in its individuals: and I do my duty again in another way by giving up to the use of the state my property and person, for the individual lives in the state. What other view will justify the facts of political life?

To repeat then: Right is the assertion of the universal will in relation to the particular will. Duty is the assertion of the particular will in the affirmation of the universal. Good is the identity, not the mere relation, of both. Right may be real, may actually exist; or be only ideal, merely thought of. So may duty. Rights and duties are elements in the good; they must go together. The universal cannot be affirmed except in the particular, the particular only affirms itself in the universal; but they should be suppressed in the good as anything more than elements, which reciprocally supplement each other, and should be regarded as two sides to one whole. It is not moral to stand on one's

called "unjust." Justice and injustice mean this, but they imply something more.

Injustice is, while you explicitly or implicity profess to go on a rule, the not going merely on the rule, but the making exceptions in favor of persons. Justice is the really going by nothing but one's ostensible rule in assigning advantage and disadvantage to persons.

What the rule is, is another matter. The rule may be the morally right. This is ideal justice. All lower sorts of law furnish each its own lower justice and injustice.

rights with the right; *i. e.*, right should not be *mere* right: nor moral to make a duty of all one's duties; *i. e.*, duty should not be *mere* duty.

We maintain the following theses. (1) It is false that you can have rights without duties. (2) It is false that you can have duties without rights. (3) It is false that right is merely negative.[8] (4) It is false that duty depends on possible compulsion, and a mere mistake that command always implies a threat; and (5) It is absolutely false that rights or duties can exist outside the moral world.

[8] Schopenhauer has developed this view with great clearness. He goes so far as to make wrong the original positive conception, right the mere negation of it.

CONCLUDING REMARKS

THE position we are now in can be put very shortly. Morality is an endless process and therefore a self-contradiction and, being such, it does not remain standing in itself, but feels the impulse to transcend its existing reality.

It is a self-contradiction in this way: it is a demand for what cannot be. Nothing is good but the good will; nothing is to be real but the good; and yet the reality is not wholly good. Neither in me, nor in the world, is what ought to be what is, and what is what ought to be; and the claim remains in the end a mere claim.

The reason of the contradiction is the fact that man is a contradiction. But man is more; he feels or knows himself as such, and this makes a vital difference; for to feel a contradiction is *ipso facto* to be above it. Otherwise, how would it be possible to feel it? A felt contradiction which does not imply, beside its two poles, a unity which includes and is above them, will, the more it is reflected on, the more be seen to be altogether unmeaning. Unless man was and divined himself to be a whole, he could not feel the contradiction, still less feel pain in it, and reject it as foreign to his real nature.

So we see that the moral point of view, which leaves man in a sphere with which he is not satisfied, cannot be final. This or that human being, this or that passing stage of culture, may remain in this region of weariness, of false self-approval and no less false self-contempt; but for the race, as a whole, this is imposssible. It has not done it; and, while man is man, it certainly never will do it.

And here we should close these Essays, since here we go beyond morality. But, that we may make the foregoing plainer, we are tempted to say something more, however fragmentary, however much in the form of an appendix.[1]

Reflection on morality leads us beyond it. It leads us, in short, to see the necessity of a religious point of view. It certainly does not tell us that morality comes first in the world and then religion. What it tells us is that morality is imperfect, and imperfect in such a way as implies a higher, which is religion.

Morality issues in religion; and at this word "religion" the ordinary reader is upon us with cries and questions, and with all the problems of the day—God, and personal God, immortality of the soul, the conflict of revelation and science, and who knows what beside? He must not expect any answer to these questions here; we are writing a mere appendix; and in that our object is to show that religion, as a matter of fact, does give us what morality does not give; and our method is simply, so far as our purpose requires, to point to the facts of the religious consciousness without drawing conclusions to the right or left, without trying to go much below the surface, or doing anything beyond what is wanted in this connection with morality.

We purpose to say nothing about the ultimate truth of religion —nothing again about its origin in the world, or in the individual. We are to take the religious consciousness as an existing fact, and to take it as we find it now in the modern Christian mind, whether that mind recognizes it or whether it does not. And

[1] Throughout the sequel I have to acknowledge my indebtedness to Vatke's book, *Die menschliche Freiheit*, 1841.

lastly, space compels us to do no more than dogmatically assert what seems to us to be true in respect of it.

That there is some connection between true religion and morality everyone we need consider sees. A man who is "religious" and does not act morally, is an impostor, or his religion is a false one. This does not hold good elsewhere. A philosopher may be a good philosopher, and yet, taking him as a whole, may be immoral; and the same thing is true of an artist, or even of a theologian. They may all be good, and yet not good men; but no one who knew what true religion was would call a man, who on the whole was immoral, a religious man. For religion is not the mere knowing or contemplating of any object, however high. It is not mere philosophy nor art because it is not mere seeing, no mere theoretic activity, considered as such or merely from its theoretical side. The religious consciousness tells us that a man is not religious, or more religious, because the matter of his theoretic activity is religious; just as the moral consciousness told us that a man was not moral, or more moral, simply because he was a moral philosopher. Religion is essentially a doing, and a doing which is moral. It implies a realizing, and a realizing of the good self.

Are we to say then that morality is religion? Most certainly not. In morality the ideal is not: it forever remains a "to be." The reality in us or the world is partial and inadequate; and no one could say that it answers to the ideal, that, morally considered, both we and the world are all we ought to be, and ought to be just what we are. We have at furthest the belief in an ideal which in its pure completeness is never real; which, as an ideal, is a mere "should be." And the question is, Will that do for religion? No knower of religion, who was not led away by a theory, would answer Yes. Nor does it help us to say that religion is "morality touched by emotion"; for loose phrases of this sort may suggest to the reader what he knows already without their help, but, properly speaking, they *say* nothing. *All* morality is, in one sense or another, "touched by emotion." Most emotions, high or low, can go with and "touch" morality; and the moment we leave our phrase-making, and begin to reflect, we see all that is meant is that morality "touched" by *religious* emotion is religious; and so, as answer to the question What is religion? all that we have said is "It is religion when with morality you have—religion." I do not think we learn a very great deal from this.[2]

Religion is more than morality. In the religious consciousness we find the belief, however vague and indistinct, in an object, a not-myself; an object, further, which is real. An ideal which is not real, which is only in our heads, cannot be the object of religion; and in particular the ideal self, as the "is to be" which is real only so far as we put it forth by our wills, and which, as an ideal, we cannot put forth, is not a real object, and so not the object for religion. Hence, because it is unreal, the ideal of personal morality is not enough for religion. And we have seen before that the ideal is not realized in the objective world of the state; so that, apart from other objections, here again we cannot find the religious object. For the religious consciousness that object is real; and it is not to be found in the mere moral sphere.

But here once more "culture" has come to our aid, and has shown us how here, as everywhere, the study of polite literature which makes for meekness, makes needless also all further education; and we felt already as if the clouds that metaphysic had wrapped about the matter were dissolving in the light of a fresh and sweet intelligence. And, as we turned toward the dawn, we sighed over poor Hegel, who had read neither Goethe nor Homer nor the Old and New Testaments, nor any of the literature which has gone to form "culture," but, knowing no facts, and reading no books, nor ever asking himself "such a tyro's question as what

---

[2] Compare (Mill, *Dissertations*, I, 70-1) the definition of poetry as "man's thoughts tinged by his feelings"; where the whole matter again is, *what* feelings? Anything in the way of shallow reflection on the psychological form, anything rather than the effort to grasp the content. All that Mill saw wanting in this "definition" was that it missed "the poet's utter unconsciousness of a listener." However, to make sure of hitting the mark, he, so to speak, set it down as hit beforehand, and in his own "definition" of poetry introduced "the poet's mind." This is much as if we were to say, "Religion is the sort of thing you have in a religious man."

being really was,"[3] sat spinning out of his head those foolish logo-
machies, which impose on no person of refinement.

Well, culture has told us what God *was* for the Jews; and we
learn that "I am that I am" means much the same as "I blow
and grow, that I do," or "I shall breathe, that I shall"; and this,
if surprising, was at all events definite, not to say tangible. However, to those of us who do not think that Christianity is called
upon to wrap itself any longer in "Hebrew old clothes," all this is
entirely a matter for the historian. But when "culture" went on
to tell us what God *is* for science, we heard words we did not
understand about "streams," and "tendencies," and "the Eternal";
and, had it been anyone else that we were reading, we should
have said that, in some literary excursion, they had picked up a
metaphysical theory, now out of date, and putting it in phrases
the meaning of which they had never asked themselves, had then
served it up to the public as the last result of speculation, or of
that "flexible common sense" which is so much better. And as
this in the case of "culture" and "criticism" was of course not
possible, we concluded that for us once again the light had shone
in darkness. But the "stream" and the "tendency" having served
their turn, like last week's placards, now fall into the background,
and we learn at last[4] that "the Eternal" is not eternal at all, unless
we give that name to whatever a generation sees happen, and
believes both has happened and will happen—just as the habit
of washing ourselves might be termed "the Eternal not ourselves
that makes for cleanliness," or "Early to bed and early to rise"
the "Eternal not ourselves that makes for longevity," and so on—
that "the Eternal," in short, is nothing in the world but a piece
of literary clap-trap. The consequence is that all we are left
with is the assertion that "righteousness" is "salvation" or "welfare," and that there is a "law" and a "Power" which has something to do with this fact; and here again we must not be ashamed
to say that we fail to understand what any one of these phrases
mean, and suspect ourselves once more to be on the scent of
clap-trap.

[3] *Contemporary Review,* XXIV, 988.
[4] *Ibid,* p. 995.

If what is meant be this, that what is ordinarily called virtue does always lead to and go with what is ordinarily called happiness, then so far is this from being "verifiable"[5] in everyday experience, that its opposite is so; it is not a fact, either that to be virtuous is always to be happy or that happiness must always come from virtue. Everybody knows this, Mr. Arnold "must know this, and yet he gives it, because it suits his purpose, or because the public, or a large body of the public, desire it; and this is clap-trap."[6]

It is not a fact that to be virtuous is always, and for that reason to be happy; and, even were it so, yet such a fact cannot be the object of the religious consciousness. The reality, which answers to the phrases of culture, is, we suppose, the real existence of the phrases as such in books or in our heads; or again a number of events in time, past, present, and future (*i. e.*, conjunctions of virtue and happiness). We have an abstract term to stand for the abstraction of this or that quality; or again we have a series or collection of particular occurrences. When the literary varnish is removed, is there anything more?[7] But the object of the religious consciousness must be a great deal more. It must be what is real not only in the heads of this person or set of persons, nor again as this or that finite something or set of somethings. It is in short

---

[5] We hear the word "verifiable" from Mr. Arnold pretty often. What is to verify? Has Mr. Arnold put "such a tyro's question" to himself? If to verify means to find in outward experience, then the object of true religion cannot be found as this or that outward thing or quality, and so cannot be verified. It is of its essence that in this sense it should be unverifiable.

[6] *Op. cit.*, p. 804.

[7] "Is there a God?" asks the reader. "Oh yes," replies Mr. Arnold, "and can verify him in experience." "And what is he then?" cries the reader. "Be virtuous, and as a rule you will be happy," is the answer. "Well, and God?" "That is God"; says Mr. Arnold, "There is no deception, and what more do you want?" I suppose we do want a good deal more. Most of us, certainly the public which Mr. Arnold addresses, want something they can worship and they will not find that in an hypostasized copy-book heading, which is not much more adorable than "Honesty is the best policy," or "Handsome is that handsome does," or various other edifying maxims which have not yet come to an apotheosis.

very different from either those thin abstractions or coarse "verifiable" facts, between which and over which there is for our "culture" no higher third sphere, save that of the literary groping which is helpless as soon as it ceases to be blind.

But let us turn from this trifling, on which we are sorry to have been forced to say even one word; let us go back to the religious consciousness.

Religion, we have seen, must have an object; and that object is neither an abstract idea in the head, nor one particular thing or quality, nor any collection of such things or qualities, nor any phrase which stands for one of them or a collection of them. In short, it is nothing finite. It cannot be a thing or person in the world; it cannot exist in the world, as a part of it, or as this or that course of events in time; it cannot be the "All," the sum of things or persons—since, if one is not divine, no putting of ones together will beget divinity. All this it is not. Its positive character is that it is real; and further, on examining what we find in the religious consciousness,[8] we discover that it is the ideal self considered as realized and real. The ideal self, which in morality is to be, is here the real ideal which truly is.

For morals the ideal self was an "ought," an "is to be" that is not; the object of religion is that same ideal self, but here it no longer only ought to be, but also is. This is the nature of the religious object, though the manner of apprehending it may differ widely, may be anything from the vaguest instinct to the most thoughtful reflection.

With religion we may here compare science and art. The artist and poet, however obscurely, do feel and believe that beauty, where it is not seen, yet somehow and somewhere is and is real; though not as a mere idea in people's heads, nor yet as anything in the visible world. And science, however dimly, starts from and rests upon the preconception that, even against appearances, reason not only ought to be, but really is.

Is then religion a mere mode of theoretic creation and contemplation, like art and science? Is it a lower form or stage of

[8] The reader must carefully distinguish what is *for* (or before) the religious consciousness, and what is only *in* it, and *for us* as we investigate it.

philosophy, or another sort of art, or some kind of compound mixture? It is none of these, and between it and them there is a vital difference.

In the very essence of the religious consciousness we find the relation of our *will* to the real ideal self. We find ourselves, as this or that will, against the object as the real ideal will, which is not ourselves, and which stands to us in such a way that, *though real, it is to be realized, because it is all and the whole reality*.

A statement, no doubt, which may stagger us; but the statement, we maintain, of a simple fact of the religious consciousness. If anyone likes to call it a delusion, that makes no difference; unless, as some people seem to think, you can get rid of facts by applying phrases to them. And, however surprising the fact may be to the reader, it certainly ought not to be new to him.

We find the same difficulty, that the real is to be realized, both in art and science. The self dimly feels, or forefeels, itself as full of truth and beauty, and unconsciously sets that fullness before it as an object, a not-itself which is against itself as this or that man. And so the self goes on to realize what it obscurely foreknows as real; it realizes it, although, and because, it is aware of it as real. And in this, so far, art, philosophy, and religion are the same.

But, as we saw, they are also different. In art and science the will of the man who realizes is not of the essence. The essence of the matter is that a certain result should be produced, that, of the unseen object which is divined to be real, a part at least should become visible, that in short, however it comes about, some element of the real should be *seen* to be realized. Here the end is the sight of the object, as such, and the will which procures that sight is not taken into account. No doubt it would be a great mistake to forget that art and science involve will, and the will of particular persons, and that it is this will which realizes the object; and that hence, since the object of science and art is at least partly identical with the object of religion, both science and art may so far be said to imply religion, since they imply the relation of the particular will to the real ideal. For suppose that the human-divine life is one process, and suppose again that art and science and religion are distinguishable elements or aspects of this one whole process. Then, if this is so, neither art nor science nor religion can exist as a thing by itself, and the two former will necessarily imply the latter. But on the other hand, though we may not divide, yet we have to distinguish; and when by an abstraction we consider one side, *e. g.*, the side of science or that of art, by itself, and take them as mere theoretic activities, then we must say that in this character neither of them is religion; and they are not religion because the will of this or that man, over against the real ideal as will, is not an element in the scientific or artistic process as such. The real ideal of science and art is not will, and the relation of my will to it falls outside them; and we must say, and we think that the reader will agree, that, so soon as the philosopher or artist is conscious of his will in relation to the real ideal, as a will which has demands on him, he ceases to be a mere philosopher or artist as such (which after all no human being is), and becomes also religious or irreligious.

To proceed, we find in the religious consciousness the ideal self as the complete reality and we have, beside, its claim upon us. Both elements, and their relation, are given in one and the same consciousness. We are given as this will, which, because this will, is to realize the real ideal; the real ideal is given as the will which is wholly real, and therefore to be realized in us.

Now nothing is easier than for a one-sided reflection to rush in with a cry for clearness and consistency, and to apply its favorite "either—or." "*If* real, how realize? *If* realize, then not real." We, however, must not allow ourselves to give way to the desire for drawing conclusions, but have to observe the facts; and we see that the religious consciousness refuses the dilemma. It holds to both one and the other, and to one because of the other, and pronounces such reflections irreligious.

In the moral consciousness we found two poles, myself and the ideal self. The latter claimed to be real, and to have all as its reality; but, for the moral consciousness, it was not thus real either in the world or in us, and the evil in us and the world was *as* real. In religion we find once more two poles, myself and the ideal self. But here the latter not only claims to be, but also is real and all reality; and yet (at this stage⁹) it is not realized either in the world or in me. It is not one pole, however, that in religion is different, but both: for morality the world and the self remained both nonmoral and immoral, yet each was real; for religion the world is alienated from God, and the self is sunk in sin; and that means that, against the whole reality, they are felt or known as what is not and is contrary to the all and the only real, and yet as things that exist. In sin the self feels itself in contradiction with all that truly is. It is the unreal, that, knowing itself to be so, contradicts itself as the real; it is the real, which, feeling itself to be so, contradicts itself as the unreal, and in the pain of its intolerable discord can find no word so strong, no image so glaring as to portray its torment.

For it really is itself, against which, in sin, it feels itself. We cannot stay to develop this doctrine, and must content ourselves with pointing out that the opposite is utterly incomprehensible. The two poles are what they are, because they are against each other in consciousness. In them the self feels itself divided against itself; and, unless they both fall within one subject, how is this possible? We have not the felt struggle of ourself against a perceived or thought external object; we have the felt struggle in us of two wills, with both of which we feel ourselves identified. And this relation of the divine and human will *in* one subject is a psychological impossibility, unless they are the wills *of* one subject. Remove that condition, and the phenomena in their specific character instantly disappear. You cannot understand the recognition of and desire for the divine will; nor the consciousness of sin and rebellion, with the need for grace on the one hand and its supply on the other; you turn every fact of religion into unmeaning nonsense, and you pluck up by the root and utterly destroy all possibility of the Atonement, when you

⁹ The thoughtful reader may at once object that here we have an incomplete account of religion. That is quite true, and we purposely delay the consideration of religion as a whole. Here we are insisting on certain elements of the religious consciousness, in order to see that they are no more than elements, which call for comprehension in something higher.

deny that the religious consciousness implies that God and man
are identical in a subject.[10]

[10] On this whole matter, and not specially with reference to religion, it is
worth while to consider the position of our philosophy. People find a subject
and object correlated in consciousness; and, having got this *in* the mind,
they at once project it outside the mind, and talk as if two independent
realities knocked themselves together, and so produced the unity that apprehends them; while, all the time, to go out of that unity is for us literally to
go out of our minds. And when the monstrous nature of their position
dawns on some few, and they begin to see that without some higher unity
this "correlation" is pure nonsense, then answering to that felt need, they
invent a third reality, which is neither subject nor object but the "Unknowable" or the Thing-in-itself (there is no difference). But here, since the two
correlates are still left together with, and yet are *not*, the Unknowable, the
question arises, How does this latter stand to them? and the result is that
the Unknowable becomes the subject of predicates (see Mr. Spencer's *First
Principles*), and it becomes impossible for any one who cares for consistency
to go on calling it the Unknowable. So it is necessary to go a step further,
and giving up our third, which is *not* the correlates, to recognize an Identity
of subject and object, still however persisting in the statement that this
identity is *not* mind. But here again, as with the Unknowable, and as
before with the two correlated realities, it is forgotten that, when mind
is made only a part of the whole, there is a question which *must* be
answered; "If so, how can the whole be known, and for the mind? If about
any matter we know nothing whatever, can we say anything about it? Can
we even say that it is? And, if it is not in consciousness, how can we know
it? And if it is in and for the mind, how can it be a whole which is *not*
mind, and in which the mind is only a part or element? If the ultimate
unity were not self or mind, we could not know that it was not mind: that
would mean going out of our minds. And, conversely, if we know it, it
cannot be not mind. All, in short, we can know (the psychological form is
another question) is the self and elements in the self. To know a not-self is
to transcend and leave one's mind. If we know the whole it can only be
because the whole knows itself in us, because the whole is self or mind,
which is and knows, knows and is, the identity and correlation of subject
and object."

There is nothing in the above which has not been before the world for
years, and it is time that it should be admitted or refuted. I think it will not
be much longer disregarded. Much against its will English thought has been
forced from the correlation as far as the identity; and, if it means to hold to
the doctrine of "relativity of knowledge," it must go on to mind or self in
some sense of the word, as this identity of inner and outer. Perhaps not
that; but if not that, then I think we must begin on a fresh basis, or else

For it is the atonement, the reconciliation (call it what you please, and bring it before your mind in the way most easy to you), to which we must come, if we mean to follow the facts of the religious consciousness. Here, as everywhere, the felt contradiction implies, and is only possible through, a unity above the discord—take that away, and the discord goes. The antithesis of the sinful and divine will is implicitly their union; and that union, in the subject, requires only to be made explicit, for the subject, by thought and will.

But for the subject it is not yet explicit; and it is only we who reflect upon the religious consciousness, that see the matter thus. That consciousness as such has not the insight that the divine will is the will of its own true and inmost self: I may know that, as a fact, in God there is the unity of the two natures; but for me God is (here at least) *only* not *my* self; the divine is an object between which and me there is a chasm; my inner self may desire it, but can only desire it as an other and a beyond. True that the object is already the identity of God and man, but man does not include me: that object is not in me, it is only for me; it remains an object, and I remain outside. And for the religious consciousness the problem is, How can I be reconciled with this will which is not mine?

And the answer is that in the object the reconciliation of the divine and human is real; the principle is there already; and in its reality, the reality of the reconciliation of the human as such, is ideally contained my reconciliation. Yes, mine is there if only I can take hold of it, if only I can make it my own; but how with the sin that adheres to me can this ever be? How can the human-divine ideal ever be my will?

The answer is, Your will it never can be as the will of your private self, so that your private self should become wholly good. To that self you must die, and by faith be made one with the ideal. You must resolve to give up your will, as the mere will of this or that man, and you must put your whole self, your

give up the attempt to have any theory of first principles. But if we do (as perhaps we may do) the latter, then let me conclude this note by observing that amongst the other doctrines which must go is the doctrine of Relativity.

entire will, into the will of the divine. That must be your one self, as it is your true self; that you must hold to both with thought and will, and all other you must renounce; you must both refuse to recognize it as yours, and practically with your whole self deny it. You must believe that you too really are one with the divine, and must act as if you believed it. In short, you must be justified not by works but solely by faith. This doctrine, which Protestantism, to its eternal glory, has made its own and sealed with its blood, is the very center of Christianity; and, where you have not this in one form or another, there Christianity is nothing but a name.

In mere morality this faith is impossible. There you have not a real unity of the divine and human with which to identify yourself; and there again the self, which is outside the ideal, is not known as unreal, and cannot be, since the ideal is not all reality.

But what is faith? It is perhaps not an easy question to answer, but in some sort it must be answered; and to neglect it as worthless or stand aloof from it as a mystery, are both wrong positions. It is easy to say what faith is not. It is not mere belief, the simple holding for true or fact; it is no mere theoretic act of judgment.[11] Everyone knows you may have this, and yet not have faith.

Faith does imply belief, but more than this, it implies also will. If my will is not identified with that which I hold for fact, I have not faith in it. Faith is both the belief in the reality of an object, and the will that that object be real, and where either of these elements fails, there is no faith. But even this is not all. When Mr. Bain, for instance, (p. 526) says, "The infant who has found the way to the mother's breast for food, and to her side for warmth, has made progress in the power of faith," we are struck at once by an incongruity. That the child who is most forward in a matter of this sort, is most likely in after life to have what

---

[11] I use belief in the ordinary sense. Of course our account of the matter is wrong if all belief is practical. This Mr. Bain (*Emotions*, 2nd ed., p. 524 and ff.) tries to show, as it seems to us, at the expense of facts, and with not sufficient success to warrant our entering on the matter.

we call faith, we see no reason to believe; that he has it already, we see is an absurdity. And we found above (p. 119) that, even in "My Station and its Duties," we could not properly speak of faith because there was there what might be called sight.

What does this point to? Does it mean that faith implies uncertainty, or defective knowledge; and that this is the reason why, where you see, you cannot have faith? No, this we think is a mistaken view, and the facts confute it. Certainly you may have faith without feeling sure of the fact; but, generally speaking, a doubt about the fact weakens faith. Nor is it the case that theoretic certainty excludes faith. If it were so, the raising of belief with doubt to belief without doubt would *ipso facto* destroy faith; and this is not so.

We cannot maintain that, when mere belief is raised to speculative certainty, the necessity for faith disappears; or further, that faith is here impossible. We must try to show the cause of the error. What can be said in its favor is this, that sight does exclude faith; and hence faith is not imagined to exist in the Paradise after death, nor, I suppose, in ecstatic vision during life. This is all consistent; but what it points to is the fact that faith is incompatible, not with such and such a *degree*, but with such and such a *kind* of knowledge. Faith is incompatible with common immediate sensuous knowing, or with a higher knowledge of the same simple direct nature; and, because our knowledge of the highest is, in religion, not thus immediate, therefore we are said to have *only* faith; and faith is, by a confusion, supposed to exclude, not one kind of certainty, but all kinds. Whence the above mistake, which, however, has a truth in it.

Why is it then that faith is incompatible with sensuous knowledge? It is because, in religious language, faith is a rise beyond "this world," and a rise in which I stay here. What does this mean? Does it mean that the object must not be a part of the visible world? It means this, and more; faith implies the rise in thought, but not that only; it implies also the rise of the *will* to the object, which is not seen but thought. And this presupposes the practical separation for me of myself and the object. In the mere theoretic rise I do not think of myself, but only of the object: in faith I must also have myself before me; I must perceive the chasm between myself, as this or that unreal part of the unreal finite world, and at the same time must perceive the ideal-real object, which is all reality, and my true reality. And it is this presupposed consciousness of absolute separation (which, in terms of space or time, we express by "this world" and the "other world") which is necessary for faith, and which survives therein as a suppressed element. Hence, where this is not, faith cannot be.

Faith then is the recognition of my true self in the religious object, and the identification of myself with that both by judgment and will; the determination to negate the self opposed to the object by making the whole self one with what it really is. It is, in a word, of the heart.[12] It is the belief that only the ideal is real, and the will to realize therefore nothing but the ideal, the theoretical and practical assertion that only as ideal is the self real.

Justification by faith means that having thus identified myself with the object, I feel myself in that identification to be already one with it, and to enjoy the bliss of being, all falsehood overcome, what I truly am. By my claim to be one with the ideal, which comprehends me too, and by assertion of the nonreality of all that is opposed to it, the evil in the world and the evil incarnate in me through past bad acts, all this falls into the unreal: I being one with the ideal, this is not mine, and so imputation of offenses goes with the change of self, and applies not now to my true self, but to the unreal, which I repudiate and hand over to destruction.[13]

[12] "True faith is no mere thought nor admission of the truth of a history." "The true Christian is not the man who knows history." "Christianity should know that faith is not merely a history or science. To have faith is nought else than for a man to make his will one with God's, and take up God's word and might in his will, so that twain, God's will and man's will, turn to one being and substance. Thereupon in the man Christ, in his passion, his dying, his death, and uprising, in his own humanity, is reckoned for righteousness, so that the man becomes Christ, that is after the spiritual man. . . . He who teaches and wills otherwise is yet in the whoredom of Babylon."—J. BÖHME.

[13] Here again the vehement expression of mysticism. "When reason tells

In one way faith is of course *only ideal*, for the bad self does not cease. Yet religion is here very different from morality. Recalling to the reader what we said as to the meaning of "evolution" or "progress" (p. 126), we say here that morality is an evolution or progress. The end, which is involved in these, is becoming realized *in* the evolution or progress, and therefore is not yet real; and so in morality we have the end presented as what claims to be real, together with the process of its realization, and that means its nonreality. Here we are not what we are, and must welcome a progress; though that means a contradiction, which again we know we are not. But for religious faith the end of the evolution is presented as that which, despite the fact of the evolution, is already evolved; or rather which stands above the element of event, contradiction, and finitude. Despite what seems, we feel that we are more than a progress or evolution, in fact not that at all, but now fully real; and this full reality of ourselves we present to ourselves as an object, and by recognizing, both by judgment and will, in that object our real self, we anticipate, or rather rise above the sphere of, progress. Ourselves being one with that object, we say we are a whole, and harmonious now. So far as we are not so, we are mere appearance; and by the standing will to negate that seeming self, we are one with the true and real self. For this point of view and in this sphere (not outside it) imputation ceases, though the bad self is still a fact; and in this sense faith remains only ideal.

But that it is in any other sense merely ideal is a vulgar and gross error which, so far as it rests on St. Paul, rests on an entire misunderstanding of him. In faith we do not rise by the intellect to an idea, and leave our will somewhere else behind us. Where there is no will to realize the object, there is no faith; and where there are no works, there is no will. If works cease, will has ceased; if will has ceased, faith has ceased. Faith is not the

thee, 'Thou art outside God,' then answer thou, 'No, I am in God, I am in heaven, in it, in him, and for eternity will never leave him. The devil may keep my sins, and the world my flesh; I live in God's will, his life shall be my life, his will my will; I will be dead in my reason that he may live in me, and all my deeds shall be his deeds.' "

desperate leap of a moment; in true religion there is no one washing which makes clean. In Pauline language, that "I have died," have in idea and by will anticipated the end, proves itself a reality only by the fact that "I die daily," do perpetually in my particular acts will the realization of the end which is anticipated. Nor does faith mean simply works; it means the works *of* faith; it means that the ideal, however incompletely, is realized. But, on the other hand, because the ideal is not realized completely and truly *as* the ideal, therefore I am not justified by the works, which issue from faith, *as* works; since they remain imperfect. I am justified solely and entirely by the ideal identification; the existence of which in me is on the other hand indicated and guaranteed by works, and in its very essence implies them.

What we have now to do is to ask, What is the *object* with which the self is made one by faith? For our answer to this question we must go to the facts of the Christian consciousness. But the reader must remember that we shall touch these facts solely so far as is necessary to bring out the connection between religion and morality. We are to keep to a minimum, and the reader must not conclude that we repudiate whatever we say nothing about.

The object, which by faith the self appropriates, is in Christianity nothing alien from and outside the world, not an abstract divine which excludes the human; but it is the inseparable unity of human[14] and divine. It is the ideal which, as will, affirms itself in and by will; it is will which is one with the ideal. And this whole object, while presented in a finite individual form, is not yet truly presented. It is known, in its truth, not until it is apprehended as an organic human-divine totality; as one body with diverse members, as one self which, in many selves, realizes, wills, and loves itself, as they do themselves in it.

And for faith this object is the real, and the only real. What seems to oppose it is, if fact, not reality: and this seeming fact

[14] By the term "human" we understand all rational finite mind. Whether that exists or not outside our planet is not a matter which concerns us, though it does touch very nearly certain forms of Christian belief.

has two forms: one the imperfection and evil in the heart, the inner self; and the other the imperfection and evil in the world of which my external self is a part. In both these spheres, the inner and outer, the object of religion is real; and the object has two corresponding sides, the inner and personal, and the external side; which two sides are sides of a single whole.

Faith involves the belief (1) that the course of the external world, despite appearances, is the realization of the ideal will; (2) that on the inner side the human and divine are one: or the belief (1) that the world is the realization of humanity as a divine organic whole;[15] and (2) that with that whole the inner wills of particular persons are identified. Faith must hold that, in biblical language, there is "a kingdom of God," that there is an organism which realizes itself in its members, and also in those members, on the subjective side, wills and is conscious of itself, as they will and are conscious of themselves in it.

If the reader will refer back to "My Station and its Duties" (p. 113), he will see that what we had there in the relative totality of the political organism, we have here once more, though with a difference. That difference is that (1) what there was finite (one amongst and against others) is here infinite (a whole in itself), and what there was in a manner visible is here invisible; (2) the relation of the particular subject to the whole was there immediate unity by unreflecting habituation and direct perception; here it involves the thought which rises above the given, and the consciousness of a presupposed and suppressed estrangement.

Here, as in the world of my station, we have the objective side, the many affirmations of the one will, the one body, the real ideal humanity, which in all its members is the same, although in every one it is different; and which is completely realized not in any one this or that, nor in any mere "collective unity" of such particulars, but only in the whole as a whole. And we have the subjective personal side, where the one will of the whole is,

[15] I need not say that here are very great difficulties. Apart from others, the relation of the physical world to the divine will is a well-known problem. But we have nothing to do with the (possible or impossible) solution of these questions. We have to keep to what is contained in the religious consciousness, and that we take to be as above.

in its unity with the conscious members, self-conscious, and wills itself as the personal identity of the universal and particular will.[16]

Such is the object, the fore-realized divine ideal; and by faith the particular man has to make that his, to identify himself therewith, behold and feel himself therewith identified, and in his own self-consciousness have the witness of it. And this, as we explained, is done by the dying to the private self as such, by the bestowal of it on the object, and by the living in the self which is

[16] By faith, and so far as faith holds, the ideal as the self, and the self as the ideal, is all that is real; and so, on the external side of my works I regard myself as, with others, the member or function of the divine whole. What falls outside, however much a fact, is still unreal. Again, on the inside, through faith I, as the mere this me, no longer am; but only I as the self-conscious personal will of the divine, the spirit of the whole, which, as that spirit, knows itself in me. On both sides, though the form is not swallowed up nor lost, yet the mere particular content of the self has for faith disappeared.

But there is a difference on the two sides, which was also there in "My Station," but the losing sight of which was there not likely to lead to confusion; while here a confusion on this head may happen, and is a serious matter. To explain—on the inside the particular self knows and feels itself now immediately one with the universal, which is the will of all selves; but on the outside, its realization in works, it is only one member of the whole, one function or set of functions which is not, and which falls outside of, other sides or sets of functions. So long as it remains on the inside, the self is not apart from other selves; it is when it comes out to act that it is forced to distinguish itself.

It is quite true that, when we act, on the inside also the whole will is for each person diverse; for it is not a universal which remains inert. It is presented in a specialized form as what is a relative "to be done" in such and such a case, which, if reflected on, is seen to be *not* other cases—but on the inner side this reflection, and hence this discrimination, does not exist. The member feels and knows itself, not as this member distinct from that member, but (since for faith the bad self is not) immediately one with the will of the entire organism. On the outside, on the other hand, the knowledge of its distinctness is forced upon it. There its realization is indeed the affirmation of the will of the whole, but the entire whole is not there; some of it is elsewhere, and, as a whole, it is realized only in the whole, which this or that man is not. In its works the self-conscious function finds that it is not other functions; it remains finite, and all possibility of the confounding the merely human with the divine is excluded.

one with the divine ideal that is felt and known as the only real self, and now too as my self. To our previous remarks on this head we have nothing to add, and must proceed to discuss more closely the relation of religion to morality.

These, as we saw, are to a certain extent the same; and the question at once arises, Has the divine will of the religious consciousness any other content than the moral ideal? We answer, Certainly not. Religion is practical; it means doing something which is a duty. Apart from duties, there is no duty; and as all moral duties are also religious, so all religious duties are also moral.[17]

In order to be, religion must do. Its practice is the realization of the ideal in me and in the world. Separate religion from the real world, and you will find it has nothing left it to do; it becomes a form, and so ceases. The practical content which religion carries out comes from the state, society, art, and science. But the whole of this sphere is the world of morality, and all our duties there are moral duties. And if this is so, then this religious duty may collide with that religious duty, just as one moral duty may be contrary to another; but that religion, as such, should be in collision with morality, as such, is out of the question.

So far religion and morality are the same; though, as we have seen, they are also different. The main difference is that what in morality only is to be, in religion somehow and somewhere really is, and what we are to do is done. Whether it is thought of as what is done now, or what will be done hereafter, makes in this respect no practical difference. They are different ways of looking at the same thing; and, whether present or future, the reality is equally certain. The importance for practice of this religious point of view is that what is to be done is approached, not with the knowledge of a doubtful success, but with the forefelt certainty of already accomplished victory.

Morality, the process of realization, thus survives within religion. It is only as mere morality that it vanishes; as an element it remains and is stimulated. Not only is strength increased by

[17] Religion in the sense of the cultus, etc., will be considered lower down.

assurance of success, but in addition the importance of success is magnified. The individual life for religion is one with the divine; it possesses infinite worth, a value no terms can express. And the bad gains a corresponding intensity of badness. It is infinitely evil, so that, for the religious consciousness, different amounts of badness are not measurable. All men are equally, because utterly, sinful. But this extreme of evil is therefore the more easy to subdue. It is not a reality against a mere ideal, but a mere fact which is contrary to the whole reality, an unutterable contradiction. Other incentives to good also come in. For the religious consciousness evil is an offense against what we love, and what loves us, not against something not real, which no one can well love. This makes evil worse, and more painful, and increases accordingly the power of good. All external control disappears, and in its place is gratitude to that which has conquered, confidence in it, and inability to be false to it.[18]

It is the same objective will, which in "My Station" we see accomplished, in ideal morality know should be accomplished, and in religion by faith believe accomplished, which reflects itself into itself on the subjective side; and thence reasserts itself explicitly as the real identity of the human and divine will. And so the content of religion and morality is the same, though the spirit in which it is done is widely different.

But all this, we may be told, though true to a certain extent, is one-sided; there is religion beyond all this. And this objection must be attended to. We have never lost sight of the fact it rests upon, although we may have seemed to do so. That fact is what some would call religion proper, the creed, the public cultus, and the sphere of private devotion. These we must now consider, but no further than we are obliged, *i. e.*, so far as the question is touched,

---

[18] We had this, too, in "My Station and its Duties." Let me remark that, if humanity is a collection, active gratitude to it is impossible, without the most childish self-delusion. Unless there is a real identity in men, the "Inasmuch as ye did it to the least of these" becomes an absurdity. And I have never heard of anyone who, owing a debt to one man, thought he could pay it by giving to another man who was *like* the first, no matter how like.

Has religious duty another content than the moral content?

Put in this way, the question is on our view of morality absurd. If anything ought to be done, then it must be a moral duty; and the notion of religious duty, as such, outside of and capable of colliding with moral duty as such, is preposterous nonsense. If it is a religious duty to be "religious," then it is also a moral duty to be religious; precisely as, if it is a moral duty to be moral, it is also a religious duty to be moral.

A better way to put the question is, Does passing from the mere moral sphere into the religious introduce a new order of duties, to take in which morality has now to be extended? That, however, is again an improper question, since, if it is right to be thus "religious," we have no business previously to narrow morality, i. e., to exclude religiousness from the ideal which morality is to realize. It seems quite plain that the sphere of morality is the sphere of practice, and the sphere of practice is the sphere of morality. There is no escaping this conclusion; and then, so far as religion is practical, the worlds of morality and religion must coincide.

What is really at issue is this, Is religion altogether practical? Is, that is to say, the theoretical element of it coordinate with or subordinate to the practical element? Does religion, like art and science, include a theoretical sphere, which in respect of its production in and by the subject is practice, but, in itself and as produced, is not so? And next, if there is such a region, how does it stand to practice? Is it subsidiary to that, or is it an end in itself, when not brought under the practical end? And then further, how in respect of such a region is morality situated?

Instead of trying to give direct answers, the best way to clear the matter will be to begin with the extreme of a one-sided view: and, first, there is an opinion which may be said simply to identify religion with orthodoxy, with the holding for true what is true. No doubt right doctrine is a very important matter, but does that make it religion? Put it to the religious consciousness, and the answer is, No. It is the belief "with the heart" that is wanted; and where that is not, religion is not. Else even the very devils would be religious; for they, as we are told, go further even than is required of them, and add to orthodoxy the fear of God.

So, in morality, a man must know what is right; but no one is moral simply because he has that knowledge. In both cases you cannot do, without knowing what you are to do; but mere knowing, apart from doing, is neither religion nor morality.

The next modification of this one-sided opinion is the view, which is all too popular, and says, "No doubt it is true that to know is not enough; action ought to follow; but, for all that, it is religon when I say my prayers, or meditate, or go to church, and that whether it goes any further, and whether anything comes of it, or not."

By denying such a doctrine we ought not to give offense to Christians. Whether we shall give offense or not is another matter. We are sorry if it is so; but nevertheless we deny the assertion and we think that on our side we have the religious consciousness[19] and the New Testament. There we do not have the love of God and man put side by side, as things which exist or can exist apart, but, where the latter fails, there fails also the former, and with it, I suppose, religion. There we are told that "pure religion" means duty to the afflicted, and the "world," by which we are not to be spotted, is hardly all spheres outside our devotions, not every region where the authority of the clergyman ceases.

We maintain that neither church-going, meditation, nor prayer, except so far as it reacts on practice and subserves that, is religious at all. Aesthetic or speculative contemplation it may be; it may be a production of the feeling which results from the satisfied religious will; but religious it is not, except so far as it means will to do: and it is not that will, except so far as it manifests itself in religious-moral acts, external or internal—acts, that is, which realize the social, ideal-social, or ideal self, or again which are means to such realization.

It is the same with morality. I may retire into my conscience, enjoy there the happiness of virtue, edify myself with, and find pleasure in, the contemplation of it in myself or others; but that by itself is surely not moral. It may be a good thing to do this, but, if so, it is a good only so far as it strengthens the will for good,

[19] I am happy to say that "religieux" has no English equivalent.

and so issues in practice. If it go beyond that, it is at best harmless; but it may be, and more often is, pernicious and positively immoral. To dwell on the satisfaction which comes from right doing need not be wrong, but it is very dangerous, it is a most slippery positon; for the moment it leads us to enjoyment which does not arise from function, or does not react to stimulate function, then, from that moment, it is bad and goes to corrupt.

If a man were to please himself with thoughts of virtue, and then go out, neglect the virtue, and fall into the vice, would that be morality? But if a man does the same by religion, there are people who call it "religious."

The true doctrine is that devotional exercises, and sacraments, and church-goings, not only should not and ought not to go by themselves, but that by themselves they simply are not religious at all. They are the isolating a sphere of religion which, so isolated, loses the character of religion and is often even positively sinful, a hollow mockery of the divine, which takes the enjoyment without giving the activity and degenerates into what may be well enough as aesthetic or contemplative, but, for all that, is both irreligious and immoral. By themselves, when religiously considered, these things are not ends at all; they are so only when they are means to faith, and so to will, and so to practice in the world.

But how is it that such one-sided views, such gross mistakes, are possible? This is not very hard to understand. And in the first place (1) both in the moral and religious will is implied knowledge, and it obviously matters for practice what a man does know. Hence correct views are wanted; and this, which so far is true, is then twisted into making religion consist in the having right opinions, or in orthodoxy. But as we have seen, the presence of the religious object for the theoretical consciousness, in any form, is not religion.

(2) The second mistake is more common. In morality what we know we feel or see, and cannot doubt. There is nothing to believe against appearances. We have a claim and the consciousness that this is satisfied or unsatisfied, but nothing beyond ourselves to hold for true; except so far as in the social object it is before our eyes. But in religion, despite of appearances, we

have to believe that something is real. We must have an inward assurance that the reality is above the facts; and we must carry that out against facts in which we cannot see the inward reality, and seem to see what is contrary thereto. It is by faith in our reconcilement with the invisible one reality that we are justified.

That inward assurance, the self-consciousness that we are one with the divine, and one with others because one with the divine, naturally does not exist without expressing itself. And moreover it is right that it should express itself because that expression reacts most powerfully upon the self-consciousness, to intensify it, and so strengthen the conviction and will in which faith consists. It is right that the certainty of identity with the divine, and with others in the divine, should be brought home by the foretasted pleasure of unalloyed union; and that in short is the rationale of the cultus. The cultus is a means to the strengthening of faith, and is an end in itself by subserving that end. As anything more and beyond it is not an end; it may be harmless, and again it may be the destruction of true religion.

And the religious community entails signs of communion, and these, as the cultus generally, entail ministers; and it is generally found more convenient to have certain persons set apart, just as again the state generally finds it convenient to support and regulate one or more religious communities.[20] These ministers, however appointed, are a means to a means to the end; and here we have the rationale of the clerical office.

You can have true religion without sacraments or public wor-

---

[20] Religious communities may be called "churches"; but churches in this sense must not be confounded with the Church proper. That is the whole body of Christ, and whether it is limited or not depends on the answer to the question whether the spirit of Christ is limited; whether it is visible or not, is answered with that answer; as also the questions whether it can be divided, reunited, and so forth. A true view of the Church is of the last importance. From that view, in our opinion, it follows that in the one Church proper there is no hierarchy, no spiritual superior, and can be none, because the spirit of Christianity excludes such things. Wherever there are ecclesiastical superiors (as it is convenient that there should be), there *ipso facto* you have a finite religious body, which, as a consequence, cannot be nor represent the Church proper.

ship, and again both without clergymen; just as you can have clergymen and sacraments without true religion. And if a part of the clergy think that they stand in a more intimate relation with the divine Spirit than the rest of the community do, then they both go against the first principles of Christianity, and moreover anyone who does not shut his eyes can see that the facts of life confute them. What Christianity, if we mistake not, tells them is that their gifts and functions being not those of others, they have the one spirit in another way from others; but when they want to go from an "other" to a "higher," then we must tell them that there are steps wanted to reach that conclusion, and such steps as Christianity cannot admit.

The sum of the matter is this. Practical faith is the end, and what helps that is good because that is good; and where a religious ordinance does not help that, there it is not good. And often it may do worse than not help, and then it is positively hurtful.

So with religious exercises, and what too exclusively is called personal piety. They are religious if they are the simple expression of, or helps to, religion; and if not, then they are not religious, and perhaps even irreligious. Religion issues in the practical realizing of the reconcilement; and where there is no such realization, there is no faith, and no religion.

Neither against the clergy, nor the sacraments, nor private devotion am I saying one word, and the reader who so understands me altogether misunderstands me. For a large number of our clergy I have a sincere personal respect, and there is scarcely any office which in my eyes is higher than that of the minister. And I recognize fully the general necessity both for private devotion and public worship. It is the abuse, and the excess of them, against which we have to protest. Whatever is the expression of the religious spirit which carries itself out in the world is religious and good, unless it goes to excess, and the excess is measured by the failure to strengthen or the weakening of the will. Just so any institution, observance, or discipline (it matters not what) which strengthens the religious will is good, provided it does so strengthen it as a whole, and is not in other ways contrary to religion and morality. The same holds good in the moral sphere; there we may have ascetic exercises which strengthen the will, and are therefore, and so far as they do that, good; but not good, or even bad, when they go beyond. But as to what in detail is legitimate or not, all this is matter of particular fact, with which we have nothing to do.

To repeat, public and private exercises are religious and good as the simple voice of, or as means to the strengthening of, the religious will. That will consists in the faith that overcomes the world, by turning it into the Christian world which for faith it is. The inner sphere of religion, which brings home to itself its assurance and its bliss, is only the inner sphere, and by itself is not religion. By itself it is not even the inner, for it is so only when it is the inner of the outer; and that outer, where faith fails, is not, and with it goes the inner as such. A sensuous or semi-sensuous gloating over the pleasures of the anticipated result is, in morals as in religion, when considered in reference to the will, a mere debauchery. Here as there it is the Hedonism which kills practice; and considered as θεωρία, it belongs to art or science, not religion at all. Furthermore, sensitiveness or intensity of the religious consciousness is no more religion than that of the moral consciousness is morality; nor again is a right perception in these matters any more than a right perception. It is religion only when the divine will, of which for faith the world is the realization, reflects itself in us; and, with the personal energy of our own and its self-consciousness, carries out both its and our will into the world, which is its own and ours, and gives us, in the feeling which results from function, that inner assurance of identity which precedes and accompanies the action of our will. And thus for religion and morality the content of the will is the same, though the knowledge and the spirit are widely different.

If this is so, then our Essays have, in a way too imperfect, yet brought us to the end, where morality is removed and survives in its fulfillment. In our journey we have not seen much, and much that we have seen was perhaps little worth the effort, or might have been had without it. Be that as it may, the hunt after pleasure in any shape has proved itself a delusion, and the form of duty a snare, and the finite realization of "my station" was truth indeed, and a happiness that called to us to stay, but was too narrow to satisfy wholly the spirit's hunger; and ideal morality brought the sickening sense of inevitable failure. Here where we are landed at last, the process is at an end, though the best activity here first begins. Here our morality is consummated in oneness with God, and everywhere we find that "immortal Love," which builds itself forever on contradiction, but in which the contradiction is eternally resolved.

> Hic nullus labor est, ruborque nullus;
> Hoc juvit, juvat, et diu juvabit;
> Hoc non deficit, incipitque semper.